WITH DUST STILL IN HIS THROAT

WITH DUST STILL IN HIS THROAT

*The Writing of B. L. Coombes,
the Voice of a Working Miner*

edited by

BILL JONES AND CHRIS WILLIAMS

UNIVERSITY OF WALES PRESS
CARDIFF

First published by the University of Wales Press in 1999

Reprinted in 2014

www.uwp.co.uk

British Library Cataloguing-in-Publication Data.

A catalogue record for this book is available from the British Library.

ISBN   978-1-7831-6149-2

Typeset by the University of Wales Press
Printed by CPI Antony Rowe, Chippenham, Wiltshire

Contents

~

Acknowledgements

~

The editors and publishers would like to express their thanks to Vivian Davies, the copyright holder of the works of B. L. Coombes, for permission to publish extracts from the works. They would also like to thank for their co-operation the staff of the Richard Burton Archives at Swansea University where the unpublished works are stored.

INTRODUCTION

> The real history of the mines ought to be written by a man still at work underground. The dust should still be in his throat as he was writing – it seemed to me – then it would be authentic. Despite my searching, I knew of no man who answered this description. Therefore, I decided to try it myself.
>
> B. L. Coombes, 'A Miner's Record – I',
> *New Writing and Daylight*, Summer 1942

At the end of a typically detailed, seemingly dispassionate and almost matter-of-fact description of a shift underground, B. L. Coombes, the most resonant voice emanating from the South Wales Coalfield in the decade 1937–47, felt compelled to tell his readers why he had become a writer. Expressed here in characteristic style, with direct, limpid prose and use of everyday language and imagery, his convictions and fundamental purpose in writing remained guiding principles throughout his life and literary career. The products of Coombes's literary mission to inform those unfamiliar with the world of mining have earned widespread praise for their authenticity, accessibility and humanity. It is perhaps inevitable that, given its resounding impact, Coombes is primarily remembered as the author of *These Poor Hands: The Autobiography of a Miner Working in South Wales* published in 1939. Yet he also published three other books on mining and a large number of articles for a wide variety of magazines and newspapers, whilst for nearly thirty years he penned a weekly column for the *Neath Guardian*. His published works themselves form only a part of his prodigious output. There also exists a large body of unpublished work which, as well as having its own intrinsic interest and value, also contributes greatly to our understanding of Coombes himself, his writings and the world in which he lived.

With Dust Still in His Throat presents, for the first time, a selection of works by B. L. Coombes that have hitherto remained unknown to the reading public.

Bertie Louis Coombs Griffiths was born on 9 January 1893 at Wolverhampton, the son of James Coombs Griffiths, at that time a grocer, and of Harriett Thompson. The precise details of Coombes's early life are unclear, but by the time Coombes was around ten years old he was living in Treharris, Glamorgan, whilst his father and uncles worked at the local Deep Navigation Colliery. At some stage, probably around 1905–6, the family (now it seems using the surname Cumbs, Cumbes or Coombes) moved again, to Madley in Herefordshire, which Coombes regularly referred to as his family's 'native' county, thereby suggesting that they may well have lived there before going to Treharris. Coombes's father became a tenant farmer in the Madley area, and Coombes himself worked on the land as a labourer, both for his father and on neighbouring farms, before spending about a year working for a local doctor as a groom.

Coombes moved to Resolven to work in the mines, probably in 1910 when he was seventeen. In September 1913 he married Mary Rogers, who was of a similar age, Mary's father being the checkweigher and lodge secretary at Ynysarwed Colliery. Mary was a local, who spoke Welsh as her first language, and Bert learned sufficient Welsh at least to be able to carry on a conversation, although there is no evidence that he ever read or wrote Welsh. In 1914 daughter Rose was born, followed in 1924 by son Peter.

In 1919 the Coombes family moved to 10 New Inn Place, Resolven, a terraced house next to a public house of the same name, where they lived until 1938. Bert subsequently became a keen reader, cricketer, and, from 1926 onwards, a violinist and a leading local member of the St John's Ambulance, subsequently training as part of the Military Hospital Reserve in Aldershot. He also acted as secretary or impromptu letter-writer for a number of local societies. He worked at various local collieries, including the Empire Colliery, Cwmgwrach, in diverse capacities: hewer, repairer, machine-man and ambulance-man. He suffered serious injuries in underground accidents in 1930 and in 1934, and witnessed the mutilation and even death of many colleagues and friends. According to his later testimony, it was one such experience, where a colleague was killed alongside him, that stimulated him to write.

Coombes began writing in the early 1930s, buying his first typewriter for £2. As noted, he was already a keen reader, and drew his most direct inspiration from writers including Robert Tressell, Lewis Grassic Gibbon, Jack London, John Dos Passos, Upton Sinclair, Sinclair Lewis, and later, Lewis Jones. He benefited from the classes run locally by the National Council of Labour Colleges: he was to write 'I owe these classes a debt I shall not forget'. He also joined (adopting the pseudonym 'Becomb') a writing circle known as the 'British Scribbler', where aspirant writers circulated stories and plays for mutual and constructive criticism, the whole enterprise having been initiated by two altruistic Oxford dons. From 1934, despite the pressures of work and family commitments and having to write his short stories, plays and a novel, 'Castell Vale', on the kitchen table, Coombes gained confidence in his abilities, and began to enjoy a measure of success. In 1935 he penned a critique of the government's Distressed Areas policy for the monthly political magazine the *Welsh Labour Outlook*, and in the same year entered a one-act play in the National Eisteddfod at Caernarfon, whilst in 1936 he was a prize-winner in an essay competition ('What Life Means To Me') run by the *Left Review*. In 1936 also, John Lehmann, the poet and editor of *New Writing*, accepted his short story 'The Flame' which was published in 1937. Lehmann was keen to discover and promote working-class writers who had not enjoyed educational advantages and he became Coombes's mentor and an important influence on the emerging writer's life (it would be to Lehmann that Coombes would later dedicate *These Poor Hands*). Coombes won another prize for an essay on the life of a colliery ambulance-man, published by the *Daily Herald* in 1937, and by this stage was sending off short stories and articles to numerous magazines and reviews. Two more of his short stories were accepted, 'Better Off' and 'Machine Man', published in 1938 in *Left Review* and *New Writing* respectively, and were well received, further feeding the interest in Coombes created by 'The Flame'. In the course of 1937 Coombes also put the finishing touches to *These Poor Hands*, sent it off to Gollancz in the autumn of that year, and it was accepted for publication in March 1938. Coombes continued to write whilst awaiting the appearance of *These Poor Hands*: he won a silver medal at the Borough of Leyton Eisteddfod in 1938, and in August of that year was approached by *Fact* magazine to write a pamphlet for their series. His contribution, entitled *I Am A Miner*, came out in February 1939, and was hailed as a 'brilliant example' of a 'worker-autobiography' in its own right. By this time the Coombes family had moved from New Inn Place to Oak Lodge, Resolven, where for the first time Coombes had a spare room, 'a place of retreat', in which he could meditate and select his material.

Coombes's star, as a writer, was in the ascendant well before the publication of *These Poor Hands*, but it was the success of this that confirmed his importance as a working-class writer, a 'miner-writer', and provided the foundation for the rest of his literary career. Published in June 1939 as 'Book of the Month' by the Left Book Club, and selling 60,000 copies immediately, it aroused widespread interest and praise for its authenticity, its understated but natural style, and its powerful and persuasive critique of capitalist control of the coal industry. The Labour politician John Strachey felt that *These Poor Hands* was a book 'which hardly anyone could read without great pleasure and without great emotion'. According to Lehmann 'B. L. Coombes' writing about the lives of the miners may have had much to do with the great stirring of national conscience which eventually made the nationalization of the mines a priority no party could withstand'. *These Poor Hands* did not make Coombes rich, and he continued to work underground, but he later said that 'it smoothed out some of the rough times we lived through'.

After *These Poor Hands* Coombes continued writing for John Lehmann, bringing out his most well-known and best short story, 'Twenty Tons of Coal', in *New Writing* at the end of 1939, the short story 'Sabbath Night' in *Folios of New Writing* in 1940 and the documentary 'The Way We Live Now' in *Penguin New Writing* 1941. He responded to Virginia Woolf's 'The Leaning Tower' with his own 'Below the Tower' in *Folios* in 1941, and provided 'A Miner's Record' in three parts for the same imprint between 1942 and 1943. Other journals to publish his work during the Second World War included *Fortnightly*, *Argosy*, *The Listener*, *New Statesman and Nation*, and *Geographical Magazine*. He wrote a weekly column for the *Neath Guardian* in late 1940–early 1941, and then again from March 1944, a regular contribution that was to continue right down to the end of 1971. Famously Coombes fronted the 'Plan for Britain' issue of *Picture Post* in January 1941, with his piece 'This is the Problem', and became an occasional contributor to the magazine thereafter.

During the hectic war years when Coombes seemed to be constantly in demand he also continued a number of larger-scale projects: he made a handful of radio broadcasts, was involved in writing scripts for documentary films and penned a sizeable section of a Liberal Party pamphlet *The Life We Want* that came out in 1944. (Although Coombes was a committed socialist, he seems never to have been an individual member of the Labour Party, and occasionally expressed his appreciation of the Liberal Party's radical tradition, as well as his endorsement of miners' leaders such as Arthur Horner who were members of the Communist Party.) In 1941 there was another house move, from Oak Lodge to Ynysgron, a small mountain farm of sixty acres at Cwmgwrach. Coombes was now a miner, a writer and a small farmer, but his literary productivity seemed to go unchecked by this new demand on his time. In 1944 his second book, a documentary treatment of the coal industry entitled *Those Clouded Hills*, and dedicated 'To the World's Workers', was published in both Britain and the United States by the Cobbett Publishing Company. The following year Penguin published his *Miners Day*, a contemporary account of mining drawing heavily on his own experiences and on local colour. In the same year there was a further change of residence: this time to the 160-acre Nantyfedwen Farm, Onllwyn, at the head of the Dulais valley, where Coombes was to remain until the end of his life.

The first years of peace brought fulfilment, and then perhaps a certain redundancy of purpose, to Coombes. In many of his writings he had campaigned for an end to private ownership in the coal industry. Coal's nationalization in 1947 he hailed with enthusiasm, but this, allied to the wide-ranging reforms of the Attlee government, seemed to signal that, at least in part, his mission as a writer had been successful. The play *Face of Coal* he co-wrote with Jack Lindsay appeared for only one week at the Scala Theatre in London in 1946. He continued to write, in *Fortnightly*, *Anvil*, *Wales*, the *Daily Worker*, and the National Coal

Board publication *Coal,* and to broadcast on radio, but, in the new era of public ownership, it was difficult to refocus the urgent evangelical edge of his earlier work as a 'miner-writer' under monopoly capitalism. The farm took up much, perhaps too much time: by the mid-1950s, when Coombes was in his early sixties, much of the land was sold. At around the same time a serious back injury suffered underground eventually led to his retirement from the mines.

Coombes did not lose his ability or appetite for writing: in 1955 he won a literary competition on the theme of international friendship organized by the *Daily Mirror,* involving a trip to Hamburg to meet with other writers. His weekly column in the *Neath Guardian* continued unchecked, dealing with topics as varied as capital punishment and international relations, the beneficial effect of cider and the changing nature of the countryside. As late as 1960 he won first prize in the Markham Memorial Competition for the first chapter of a novel. But after this date the weekly *Guardian* column was his only output. Attempts to find a publisher for a second autobiography, 'Home on the Hill' completed in 1959, came to nought, a fate which also befell the novel 'The Singing Sycamore' written in the 1950s. In 1963, at the age of seventy, Bert Coombes was honoured by the National Union of Mineworkers (South Wales Area) for 'outstanding contributions to working-class literature'. In 1970 his wife Mary died, and Bert too succumbed on 4 June 1974, having reached eighty-one years of age. He was buried alongside his wife in the graveyard at St David's Church, Resolven, where they had been married over sixty years before. Their joint tombstone was carved as an open book, with Coombes described, according to his own wishes, simply as 'Bert Lewis Coombes (Author)'.

After Coombes's death Nantyfedwen Farm remained in the Coombes family, with a grandson, Viv Davies, son of Bert and Mary's daughter Rose, continuing to live there. In 1994, encouraged by the Swansea-based writer Alun Richards, Viv Davies deposited a collection of his grandfather's papers in the South Wales Coalfield Archive, located at the University of Wales in Swansea. These consist of four boxes of manuscripts, including drafts of short stories, plays, novels, a diary, radio scripts, a substantial autobiography written twenty years after the appearance of *These Poor Hands*, a scrapbook of letters and press cuttings, and some copies of journals in which he had published articles. The condition of the surviving material varies. Many of the drafts are incomplete, are typed on the back of other items, or have defied identification, the inevitable consequence of Coombes's recycling strategy for saving paper. Some pages seem to have been left untouched since Coombes typed them whilst others show evidence of several revisions.

From the beginning it was intended that this should be an anthology of previously unpublished writing by Coombes. To our knowledge, none of the material contained in this collection has already appeared in print, although where occasional passages bear a close resemblance to published work this has been noted. From the wide variety of material contained within the archive, selections have been made of four different types of writing: autobiography ('Home on the Hill'), short stories, a novel ('Castell Vale'), and a 'war diary'. Although written later than the other three works featured, 'Home on the Hill' is presented first because Coombes is best known as an autobiographer and because of the new biographical insights it offers. The context and provenance of each work is described in the introductions to each section of the book. Understandably this selection represents only a fraction of the hundreds of thousands of words contained in Coombes's papers. None of his plays or radio scripts have been reproduced here, in part because many were broadcast, and also because of the relatively stilted appearance that many plays have in text form. A complete novel, entitled 'The Singing Sycamore', has been omitted due to a desire to retain it intact for possible future publication. Other materials, including letters of appreciation from readers and drafts of published work, have been used to inform our understanding of Coombes, and have been cited where appropriate in our other writings upon him. A short piece entitled 'My Life from Childhood' written late in life by Mary, Coombes's wife, was given serious consideration for inclusion in this volume, but the fact that it is incomplete eventually necessitated its exclusion.

The material contained in this anthology contributes to our understanding of Coombes, his society and his literary and stylistic development in distinct ways. First, it enables us to flesh out the details of his life, many of which were largely concealed in *These Poor Hands*. We learn, particularly from the autobiography 'Home on the Hill', much more about his last year in Herefordshire, about the reasoning behind his migration to Resolven, and we discover something of his earlier residence in Treharris. This work also shows much more clearly the extent to which Coombes manifestly recycled episodes from his own life in his fictional works. Two of his best short stories, 'The Flame' and 'Machine Man', are here revealed to be fictionalized reconstructions of actual experience.

The extracts selected also allow us to trace more fully his development as a writer and set Coombes's published writing in a broader and more comprehensive context. From the evidence of the novel 'Castell Vale' and the short stories he penned as 'Becomb' we may judge that Coombes's initial aim may well have been to become primarily a writer of fiction rather than non-fiction. These early fictional works were among the first things he wrote, and they reflect Coombes's efforts to develop his own style, one that he 'could wear like a skin', as he put it. At their best they show how far Coombes was succeeding in marrying his style and purpose; he always insisted on the importance of humour and of clarity, simplicity and directness of expression in order to reach the widest audience. His accounts of horrific accidents and experiences underground, or of injustices suffered by mining families are made all the more effective by their lack of sentimentality or outraged rhetoric. In places the extracts can also reveal less felicitous writing as well as more fundamental constraints on the author's part, especially as far as fictional writing is concerned. Nevertheless, these defects do not seriously devalue the texts; rather they enable a more comprehensive assessment of Coombes's strengths and limitations as a writer. Coombes was at his best when writing about subjects with which he was familiar, and most comfortable when writing documentary works. However, he lacked sustained creative power to imagine experiences, thoughts and feelings of which he himself had no prior knowledge or had not witnessed. Coombes possessed talent and ability as a writer, but it is arguable whether he would have achieved lasting success as a novelist and a short-story writer.

A further rewarding aspect of the material is its detailed and perceptive commentary on the mining communities of his adult years. Indeed, although all the works included here reflect Coombes's central motivation of portraying and discussing conditions in the British mining industry during his lifetime, they also reveal his interest in providing a more varied commentary on the life and people of the mining communities in south Wales than that which emerges from much of his published work. Coombes was recording his own and his community's opinions upon, and experiences of, a wide variety of subjects: he was articulating a rounded social history of life in mining communities during an eventful time. One of the chapters of 'Home on the Hill' not reproduced in this anthology contains this gem of a description of the famous 'jazz' or 'gazooka' bands of the miners' strikes of the 1920s:

> During 1926 and through the slack years afterwards folk seemed happy to make their own fun. Carnival bands were organised in almost every street and one mining village had twenty six bands, all drilling and properly dressed. In some cases undressed would be a better term, but that was always for the male bands . . . reversing the usual complaint. A couple of these bands featured the Cannibals. About a score of coffee coloured miners, with no apparent clothing except grass skirts, and waving improvised spears which they thrust at any girl they judged would give a satisfactory squeal, padded along behind a massive miner whose stomach showed proof of a well beered past. This waddling leader was the cannibal king. In the centre of the group was a disconsolate individual in soiled white dungarees. He was the captive planter going most unwillingly to make a savoury stew. Behind it all were four more savages carrying on long poles across their shoulders a cooking pot which would have warmed most of the food available in that village at that lean time.

This anthology is also valuable because it strengthens our awareness of the political purpose of Coombes's writings. 'The War Diary of a Welsh Miner' provides direct and immediate reaction to national and international events, and 'Home on the Hill' allows Coombes to review the development of the south Wales coal industry and its communities in the post-war period, and to assess the record of the nationalized industry. In so doing he offers us first-hand testimony of a quality only rivalled by oral histories.

Many readers of this anthology will not already be familiar with the works of B. L. Coombes. In attempting to provide an insight into the ethos, quality and variety of his writing, we hope that this work will inspire such readers to go on to familiarize themselves with his other works. Coombes's world is now past. Coal is no longer King in south Wales and, in the twenty-first century, coalfield society has become almost exclusively an object of historical enquiry. The writings of B. L. Coombes will, however, continue to provide readers with clear insight into the lived experiences of the people of that unique society. In 1943, the Communist president of the South Wales Miners, Arthur Horner, wrote to Coombes to express his appreciation for Coombes's work. He observed: 'It is essential that those who understand the hopes and fears of their own class, shall express these feelings in a manner which can be easily understood by people outside such experiences.' We shall shortly all be 'outside such experiences' as were enjoyed and endured by Bert Coombes and his fellow workers, but we may remain thankful that Coombes in particular had the gift to express them in such a vivid, direct and human fashion.

Bill Jones and Chris Williams
Cardiff

HOME ON THE HILL:
AN AUTOBIOGRAPHY
(extracts)

INTRODUCTION

When *These Poor Hands* was published in 1939, Bert Coombes was forty-six years old. Twenty years later, retired from both mining and, more or less, farming as well, he attempted his second autobiographical volume, 'Home on the Hill', which runs to twelve chapters and a total of 120,000 words. Coombes contemplated its publication, and, in 1960, was advised by John Lehmann to approach Gollancz, but no correspondence to suggest that he took any further steps has been located. Unfortunately, Coombes, by this time in his late sixties, may have lacked the ability to sustain a narrative of such length: some of the chapters are weakly structured, and others become side-tracked by issues at a tangent to their main theme.

The best, and roughly one-sixth of the original manuscript, is presented here: all of the first chapter, the vast bulk of the second and third, and about half of the eighth. These fundamentally separate essays each have their own value. In Chapter One Coombes utilizes his familiar 'documentary' style to introduce his world, and to reflect briefly upon the course his life has taken. In Chapter Two he describes his last year, as a boy, living in Herefordshire, and in Chapter Three he provides a series of vignettes on the dangers of underground work, in the process revealing that some of his most renowned short stories were based on his own experiences. Chapter Eight contains Coombes's most sustained commentary on the objective of the nationalization of the coal industry and the fortunes of that industry after 1947.

The chapters not selected for publication include material on, amongst other things, working life underground, Coombes's involvement with the St John's Ambulance, his enthusiasm for the violin, and his experiences as a small farmer from the 1940s onwards. They contain occasionally magnificent cameos shedding light on many aspects of life in the Neath valley, and, by implication the South Wales Coalfield, from the Great War to the 1950s.

Chapter One

~

WE did not have one minute to spare. The whistle sounded, and we hurried out from the darkness, through the clouded steam which reminded us of washing day at home, and scrunched through the coal dust to the turnstiles at the lamproom. There, weight and eagerness won, and I was soon inside. I slid my ambulance box through a shutter, calling to the attendant to replace the stuff used during the shift, and hooked my lamp in the stand at its number.

Check number four hundred safely in my pocket I hurried downwards amongst the crowd. Some could linger but I had less than twenty minutes to change my appearance, and become a normal, clean human being. Eight minutes later, after shouting hurried messages to mates on the day shift going upwards, I was holding my pit boots against the revolving brushes and hurriedly undoing buttons at the same time. With the grimed clothes hanging neatly in my locker and with towels over my shoulder I picked my place beneath the showers.

The pit-head bath was full of naked and chattering males of various ages. Few better advertisements for nudism than these baths are possible. Almost every bare body there was slim and well shaped. Very few pit men are ever podgy; their work and bending see to that. New energy and cheerfulness stir our bodies as the hot shower sluices the coal dust downwards in black streams. Some start to sing and check the melody sharply as a mate slips his hand through the division and turns on the ice-cold water.

This has been one of the great alterations in our living for now we can travel without soiling the clothes of other people. In this, and many other areas the baths and canteens were in action years before the industry was nationalised. It was a belated adoption of the ideas from the Sankey Commission.[1] It is the greatest easement which has ever come to the miners' wives. When I came home clean for the first time my wife could scarce believe it.

Yet, like most humans we were suspicious. Even after all these years some few will not use the baths. Just before the opening we slyly inspected the big building, and some were not pleased. The shower cubicles had narrow divisions. Buller, who now strides alongside me with his bath towel rolled in a bundle and his powerful body birth naked was emphatic then.

'What do they think we are, hey?' Buller demanded. 'Think we're going to bath in a place like that where everybody can see? There ought to be canvas to make it more private.' Today no one bothers even to put his towel in position when moving from one section to the other. Yet that is the way of us. When the new type of lamp stands were put in and each had to place his lamp on its number there was a couple of days in which we scrambled and collided. Again there were loud complaints, almost to the threat of striking, but it works smoothly and swifter now. One reason, of course, is that most of us have trains or buses to catch and the quickest want the stolid ones to hurry for their convenience.

We opened our baths during the blackout. The roof was mainly of glass. That complicated things. They placed one miner's lamp at the end of a cubicle row and nearly a hundred miners had to undress by that glimmer; or dress if they were in the clean section. Short of time again, and also short of light, there was complete confusion. With the newness of community bathing still upsetting us one went under the showers without taking off his vest and wondered what was the matter with his skin. Several put both legs into one section of their pants; and at one end of the row two men put a foot each into the same pants and a fight was almost started about the right ownership.

Dried and dressed I feel alert and confident. A mate has placed a cup of hot tea and a cake ready for me while he goes to explain the filling of an income tax claim form to an older man. This mate is 'real hot' on income tax. We have our experts on various things and they are competent and helpful. I have known a couple who made a life study of the compensation laws. Their father was not

[1] The Royal Commission on the Coal Industry, 1919, was known as the 'Sankey Commission' after its Chairman, Lord Justice John Sankey (1866-1948).

treated fairly after an accident and ever since they have watched
for any loophole and guided any one who was injured at work –
and that means an army in numbers every year.

I can relax briefly because I can see our bus through the window
and the driver is sitting near me. When he is ready he will signal.
We are often prevented from using the canteens of other workers
but the miners' canteens make no distinctions. All are welcome to
rest and refresh themselves and watch the forms and movements
of the four very pretty girls who wait at the tables. It is ten to seven
on a May morning. The driver stretches, stands up, points at the
clock and says: 'O.K. Private Tour. Time to go.'

So out we go and start away. That Private Tour joke is a
reminder of what happened a few weeks earlier and I was the only
one to start from this canteen. We left it late and hurried out, and
swiftly away. We eased up at the first stop but none of the waiting
people signalled or attempted to get on. We had five stops in that
two miles travelled before changing and the same indifference was
shown at each stop. When I got off at the point where another
main road crosses I had been pondering why these folk, so
obviously going to the factories, had not used the only bus going
that way for an hour. I crossed in front and looked at the
destination plate. For some reason they had forgotten to change
that plate since the last trip and it signalled clearly . . . 'Private
Tour. Not for service passengers'.

So I had ridden alone in solitary state – in a thirty-two seater. I
walked to my waiting place, after pointing it out, and left the
driver and conductor thinking up excuses. Ever since I have been
known to the drivers as 'Private Tour'.

This morning there is no mistake and we soon have our seats full.
Buller has been riding with us and he gets off at the third stop. His
going seems to be welcomed by a slight and pale-faced man who
had been crushed into a few inches whilst Buller had banged his
sixteen stone hard on the same seat. To ease things Buller had
leaned more over to get a good look at the paper which the other
was trying to read. Buller got slightly excited, squeezed the reader
into an even smaller space and pointed to the back page: 'He's
going then,' he said it emphatically, 'you put your shirt on him.
They've kept him for it.' A look of agony twisted the reader's face,
he turned to protest, and met full mouth a cloud of Franklyn's
Strong which Buller had just puffed from that fierce pipe. Some of

the women turned to the back page of their paper hurriedly and Buller's victim was saved from extinction because the bus started to slacken speed and Buller got up. He turned by the door and called to me:

'So long, butty. See you at the assizes.'

The young woman sitting next to me had a minute before given me a cigarette and we had lighted up together. A hard, bed-warm thigh had been pressed against mine. Now it was sharply withdrawn. Several passengers peeped fearfully round at me and I was labelled as dangerous from that moment. Doubtless they would have liked to know what crime I had committed. So would I. Buller stood on the pavement and with his big body and beaming smile he reminded me of Will Lawther.[2] I met our then President in the bar at the Scala Theatre, London. In collaboration with Jack Lindsay I had a play running there some years before.[3] Very suspicious and silent now we moved on. Thirty human beings meeting another day. Thirty minds concerned with problems. Some married, eating, and even sleeping, alongside another human in the limit of physical intimacy, yet each holding all through the years a secret chamber in the mind that the other cannot penetrate. Man can go into the underground and probe the mysteries in the heart of creation. He can fly like a bird and send rockets to circle the sun, but he cannot probe the real thoughts of that person who lives with him through his lifetime.

Fifteen years ago there would have been no women going to work here in the early morning, no clean miners riding home. The men would have been coal black, and girls, if they wanted work, had to go away to the cities. That way the pattern of our lives has changed for the better.

Nature made this Vale of Neath in a wide and lovely situation. It is sullied now, by the sloveliness of greedy man. Rich minerals were under the ground, they paid men poorly for their skill in getting these riches to daylight; and when they were worn out they left them like the huge slag tips were left, without any consideration.

---

[2] Will Lawther, President of the MFGB / NUM, 1939–54.

[3] Co-authored by Lindsay and Coombes, *Face of Coal*, a 'documentary play', ran for a week in March 1946.

As we neared our changing place a train rushed down the railway line. The track is edged from the mountain side so the train runs easily along a slight gradient. Along that line I came about forty years ago.[4] I was a youth then, stirred by that desire which seems the national trait of the English. They all seem to think that far off fields are greener: and that the end of the rainbow is just past their horizon.

Had I not come on that train would my life have been easier or happier? Many have come here under similar conditions and most ask themselves that question in later years. Then they cannot return . . . it is too late. We came from rich, warm land and a stolid way of life to the more friendly people with a grimmer background. Most of us settled and made friends, as I did, for we were made welcome. I had a special chance because some of my schooling was at Treharris before my parents went back to their homeland and a small farm.[5] I knew the smell and sound of mining as a boy. I had watched the crowds of coal-grimed men coming home and had failed to recognise my own father when he was in pit clothes. I had seen many carried to their homes, and had sat up in bed many nights to watch the glowworm-like crowding of tiny lights near the pit top as the men waited to go down. Somewhere in me was the longing to go back amongst those dangers.

So when I felt almost a man at a strong sixteen, or nearly seventeen, I travelled that way again, in reverse. Away from the good lands, up into the steep valleys, on past Treharris where I looked longingly out at the streets I remembered and the places made rosy by school excitements, and over the crests to the end of the Neath Valley. There I had stayed gaining years and experience, and finally a young wife who like myself was under twenty, but from a good home, and quite a worker.

I had joined in trade union work, in cricket and football: in their singing and play acting: their chapels and orchestras, and their ambulance training. Even there our energy had made every day full of interest. We had seen the loaded coal trucks standing still for weeks. Had months without any work or pay and sat around

---

[4] Coombes moved from Herefordshire to Resolven in about 1910.
[5] Coombes lived in Treharris *c.*1903–5.

playing tippit with a button.[6] I had carried my plate to the soup kitchen and soled my only pair of shoes with old motor tyres. That, after we had stinted to save for years while I had worked double shifts in the colliery. With all our savings gone I had joined the long queues around the chapels waiting for the relieving officer and knowing full well the snarling answers we would get. Also what little relief we did have was for our wives and children only, and that on loan which had to be paid back. After we restarted there was a special line added on our pay docket for some years: 'Relief repayment'.

I might have avoided those times had I not ventured on that journey. Yet every experience is valuable and I found what grand material was in the miners of those days. They would die for a principle. They stood up for their beliefs even when their job, their living, and their homes might be sacrificed. To be a miners' committee-man in those days meant they were putting all they had in jeopardy. Things seem much different now for the unions have greater power and in that easing the fine spirit of the veterans that I knew has fizzled away in the present generation and union activities.

As a very young man I listened at the street corners and went to the meetings. Had I not been daily amongst them I could not have realised how nationalisation was the germ of their hopes in those bitter days. There could be no surrender to the tyranny of the owners, and managements, that controlled in that period but the time must come when the mines would be the property of the nation, the men who got the coal would have a say in the working of it, and better times would come for all. The Sankey Commission had condemned the acting owners and their day must surely pass. Through those years I helped to canvass for the Labour Party. Some of the folk who refused even to read our pamphlets then are now important members and councillors for that same party. The Labour Party has become respectable, it can offer a career and honours. Of late years it has gone forward eagerly . . . to higher incomes, titles, and snobbery. The silk hat has replaced the cloth cap.

---

[6] Tippit: OED: 'A game of chance in which an object hidden in a player's hand is to be detected.'

Yes, we believed in the Labour Party then and in nationalisation. The pioneers of both ideas would have kept their sincerity but they were mostly worn out by the conditions. Their work brought results but they were too weary to carry the torch farther. Circumstances made it possible for me to take a more effective part in nationalisation than most of them and so it may be that my disappointment is sharper. In a period when we were the chosen generation, that could have made the decade bright in political and industrial history, the human element failed to accept its task and so betrayed its forbears. Anyway, our first journey is not yet ended so we can talk about failures in another chapter.

A group of opencast workers, Irishmen, are waiting with me for the fresh bus. They grunt but never seem to talk. They pull their heads down into the collar of duffel coats which have the name of their employer stamped plainly on them. Two have turned to face the brick wall as if weary of our world. A muddy jeep rattles down the hill, stops, and a stout, middle-aged man steps out. He again is Irish, but he can talk, and does so loudly. He is a foreman and to show his authority strides back and fore along the pavement, gesticulating like an actor on the stage. He shouts about cables, welding, and drag lines. They grunt agreement in unison. He climbs back into the jeep, then suddenly remembers to throw them the key of the canteen, and adds, 'Begod. And it's awkward it is. Some bugger have pinched all the sugar.' One kicks the wall savagely, the others groan like wounded men as he drives away. Our bus swings in and dejectedly they climb aboard, the big name on their muddied backs marking them as if they had been bought.

It is uphill for four miles and the valley slips away below us. Big coal laden lorries from the opencast squeal downward protesting at the gripping brakes. A few farmhouses make white blotches on the great expanse of mountain land. Herds of ponies scamper away as we near their grazing. We drive alongside huge stretches from which the coal has been taken and the overburden replaced.[7] New wire and concrete posts make excellent fencing around it but despite the good manuring and cultivating the grass is weak, and reeds are the most plentiful growth. Probably because the natural draining has been disturbed.

---

[7] Overburden. OED: 'The overlying waste which has to be removed in quarrying or mining to get at the deposit worked.'

Quite near the summit we see three large mining villages, built right in the open to meet the wind. Each village has its monument, a giant slag tip, to keep it company. Nearer our road are other tips in a long black line with crane arms pointing upwards and a deep gulch showing across the slope. That is the opencast. They are clearing the upper seams and the local miners, working underground, can hear the cranes rattling and they do not enjoy it. They do not feel secure. The shooting disturbs their roof and water seeps through more frequently.[8] The eight 'sunshine miners' as the colliers term them, get off at the crossroads and with lowered heads and dragging feet stumble across the rough grass towards the cranes.

With the sight of those close huddled houses alongside the tips I think of my years in the valley below. We had a house like that for years and counted ourselves lucky.[9] I must have added something to those tips. How many years have I imitated the moles? A little more than forty. All right, say an average of two hundred shifts a year for forty years. That is eight thousand times into darkness and danger, away from the sweet air and sunshine. Putting my filling work, apart from all other, as five tons a day that means forty thousand tons of coal or stone loaded and sent out.

Thirty years as the skilled ambulance man in the colliery. Carrying a first aid case and attending to the injured when a call came to suspend my usual job. I believe I could assess at least one slight injury every day and a more serious one every week. Quite a few hundred journeys to various towns and villages with injured men. Very often through wintry weather and along dangerous roads. Usually in the night also, to disturb some wife or mother from her sleep with the homecoming of a badly injured person . . . if it was not worse than that.

Yes, the slighter injuries stayed at work. Slighter? I went to one man who had the end of three fingers and the three nails torn off. After being bandaged he would go on working. A close friend of mine came across often during the shifts for me to pull bits of bone from one finger. It had been smashed. He kept on working but the bits of bone worked out for weeks. During the last ten

---

[8] By 'shooting' here Coombes means shot-firing or blasting.
[9] Coombes is referring here to 10 New Inn Place, Resolven, where he and Mary lived from 1919 to 1938.

years the reported accidents have averaged about two hundred and twenty thousand each year. Time has been lost for that number. Probably a greater number were never reported.

Dust. If the fog drops on these areas a large number of the men are in torture. At one period one man every week was permanently disabled by dust at one colliery – out of less than a thousand men. I have known the men in whole families wiped out by dust disease and dying in agony. Yet the amazing part is that although some men are finished before they are twenty-five, and sometimes when they have been a distance away from the dusty places, others will work all through a long life in the dustiest districts and not be affected. Is there something different in their lung tissues or in the way they breathe . . . or is it family history? I ask this because I have noticed that native families seem to succumb quicker while the ones fresh from the country or one generation away seem to avoid the disease for a longer time. To watch those affected is a saddening thing and outsiders do not seem to understand.

For ten years I drove a coal cutting machine, the most dusty of mining tasks. I had years as a collier, more years as a repairer, and was always at a dusty job. Yet even now the X-ray shows no sign of any dust accumulation. Has the good food and sweet air of my youth helped to strengthen my resistance? Added to that even when we were living in a mining street we longed and saved for a home in the fresh air away from the streets. We were the ones with our hearts always hoping for some quiet home and the lonely places.

It seemed a vain dream when strikes used up all our savings. Yet it came true. In the bedroom of that miner's house, on an ancient and damaged typewriter, a book was written which became the Book of the Month and was selected as one of the most important in the long history of English Literature.[10] After that we got our

---

[10] Coombes is referring here to *These Poor Hands*, the Left Book Club's 'Book of the Month' for June 1939, and cited as one of the 'more prominent' autobiographies of the twentieth century in William J. Entwistle and Eric Gillett, *The Literature of England AD 500–1960: A Survey of British Literature from the Beginnings to the Present Day* (London, Longmans, 1943), 255.

sweet and quiet home, but we stayed to work and mingle with the people and the ways we knew, as we will stay until the end.[11]

I get off the bus at another crossroads and walk along a hard road. That way, exactly, the Roman legions marched on their journeyings between Neath and Brecon. Last year, a little farther on, we found a stone pick which the experts thought was dropped nearly two thousand years ago. Farther on our hard road parts with the straight Roman Way, we circle the place where their soldiers rested in camp, and can hear the crash of a great waterfall, dropping into a chasm over eighty feet. Not very far away Madame Patti had her castle built at Craig-y-nos – The Rock of the Night.[12] She thought it her ideal home.

Fifty yards along a bridge crosses a stream which has not long escaped from its mountain womb. It is clear and sparkling. It sings a low song as it moves gently along, quite unaware that in a few minutes it will be bruised and all a'froth because it has tumbled over those eighty-foot-deep rocks. Yet in its murmuring innocence it is important for it divides two counties and also two ways of life. On the one side the coal measures end as the limestone comes in. After that the farming life starts, although it is hard and un-generous as the rocks which are always only a few inches beneath the poor grass.

Here stands a long, white-walled house.[13] A house which was old long before the trees which guard it like green soldiers were the tiniest shoots. Yet it has grown old gracefully because it has been cared for and been accompanied by that half acre of garden with its strawberry beds, fruit trees, and rose-covered arches. Some hens chuckle their alarm as a dog barks. The birds continue their spring song and a plume of grey smoke drifts up towards a blue sky. The smell of ham cooking comes to meet us. The doors and windows, painted sharply red, are wide open and the big dog sidles towards us, his wagging tail an apology for that warning

---

[11] In 1938 the Coombes family moved to Oak Lodge, Rheola, just outside Resolven. They remained there until 1941, when they moved to Ynysgron Farm, Cwmgwrach.

[12] Adelina Patti (1843–1919), the famous soprano, owned and had rebuilt Craig-y-Nos Castle, Breconshire.

[13] Coombes's home from 1945 to his death in 1974, Nantyfedwen Farm.

bark. He knows his friend has returned and if he could speak he would surely say:

'Come on in. You are very welcome at the Home on the Hill.'

Chapter Two

~

NOT often as a patient but because of other activities I have had more to do with doctors than the average worker. Most of them have been splendid fellows, and I have noticed that these have always had other interests besides the human body. Doctors should not live on diagnosis alone. These have been good in drama, politics, music or possibly fishing. I knew a couple who were very much more interested in farming than surgery and I was very fond of one who would have made a great actor, but we would have lost a fine doctor. The other interests seem to keep them more natural and friendly. That assessment would leave about forty per cent who . . . but we'll have the happy memories first.

My earliest memories were of doctors in Treharris. Here there was a group surgery financed by the miners' stoppages from their pay. This surgery was about a mile from school and it needed the master's permission before one could go there with a message in the morning. Of course, we never returned to school until the afternoon. There was never any difficulty about messages. We could invent them ourselves. If we fetched pills for some imagined ailment in our home they came nicely for playing tippit or 'birds in the bush'. One boy had a weekly visit to fetch castor oil. When they queried the amount he was using he said his father liked to have his working boots soft and castor oil was the only stuff he found suitable.

As the pit was very warm my father drank about three quarts of cold tea every shift. If there was any tea in the pot it was always poured into a spare tea jack.[1] A girl cousin of about my age used

---

[1] A tea jack was essentially a water bottle with a cork stopper.

to come daily to play with me. One night she mistook the jack and took a long swig of paraffin instead. Everyone thought she must die and I galloped off for the doctor. The one on duty then was very stout and elderly. He did not want to hurry up those steep hills but by urging, dragging, and pushing him, I got him there in record time. He almost needed medical attention then, more than the girl anyhow, for she was quite all right. I think the drink did her good for she developed into a very handsome girl. I thought I must have saved her life and by her affection afterwards she must have felt the same. The doctor had other ideas I think for he used to glare at me and growl every time afterwards when I could not avoid getting close to him. When we moved away to Herefordshire I became so healthy that doctors and their calling were unknown in our lives.[2] Until one day, when an old woman living down the road had a stroke. She was our nearest neighbour and I was sent on a bicycle for the doctor. He lived about six miles away. I had not been there before but I found the village and the surgery without much delay. The surgery was closed but the big house was alongside and I went up to the door of a long conservatory. When I knocked a voice said 'Hallo'. It was one of the loveliest voices I had ever heard. There was a caress in it, almost the promise of a kiss. It was a welcome to a loved one. I grew hot all over and stammered that the doctor was wanted. No one answered and I saw no one. I knocked again – and again came that soft, seductive, 'Hallo'. Almost trembling with surprise at this mysterious greeting I turned my head and saw the parrot in a cage. Why do they not train thousands of parrots like that and sell them to lonely bachelors?

I went farther in then and knocked on another door. This brought a human answer and she was no reason for retreat either. In those days slim girls looked very attractive in black dress, white apron and tiny white cap on top of a good head of uncropped hair. That appearance did not ease my nervousness. I told my message and she considered me well. Then another of similar size and dress came up to look over her shoulder and yet a third maid stood about a yard behind. They seemed in a difficulty then the first one stated:

---

[2] Coombes and his parents moved from Treharris to Madley in Herefordshire *c.* 1905–6.

'I don't know . . . but p'raps I'd better tell him. Will you go to the surgery door? I'll unlock it.'

Very quickly to get away from such a crowd of femininity, for as the only child this was a strange experience to me, I went by the surgery door. A couple of minutes later there was some expert coughing and gasping the other side of the door and the doctor marched out. I stepped back more into the opening for he was an imposing figure. He stood about six foot three and was very broad. Added to that he was still wearing a high silk hat, a thick brown coat with a wide velvet collar, a big white scarf and spats . . . with ordinary clothes as well.

'You are from . . .', he spoke in a voice to match.

I confessed that I was.

'You want me to come at once? At once you said?'

I confessed feebly to that misdemeanour also.

'Ha. You do, do you? And how am I to get there my dear sir? Tell me that, hey? Tell me that.'

I suppose that was the first time anyone had called me 'dear sir' and it encouraged me. I said the road seemed all right when I came over it.

'Ha. All right, is it? Do you expect me to walk, hey? Do you know, sir, that I haven't even started on my regular patients yet? Damn these townees. What good are they? Tell me that. Like children with horses. No more townees for me, my dear sir, no more.'

Off he marched back into the house while I stood wondering what was happening. Hardly had he disappeared when two of the girls came out quietly. They wanted to know what he had said, then I heard the particulars. Either he had been unlucky, or he was very difficult to suit, but he had three different grooms within the last year and the last one had left in anger that morning and had not looked back. They were all married men, living in a cottage which went with the job and were supposed to be in charge of the garden as well. They had all been sent there by his sister who lived in Hereford city. They may have been gardeners but not one of them was a horseman. I knew I could handle anything in that line. I had helped to break young horses and for many months had been working three young horses abreast. It was near my sixteenth birthday but I was as big and quite as strong as an average man. I could not understand the deadlock.

'Why don't he drive himself?' I asked.

Two of the maids, and they were very pretty, had been quietly standing alongside, looking as sympathetic as they thought the occasion needed. They were surprised at my query.

'Drive himself? Why, he's frightened to death of the horses. He won't go near them if he can help it.'

This big, domineering doctor afraid of his own horses. He shrank to midget size in my opinion at once. I also saw the solution.

'Then I'll drive,' I stated.

They looked at me silently for a minute, then the oldest, her name was Helen I found out later, said:

'They're wild horses. That's what was the matter.'

'I'll manage that.' I was confident. 'Will you tell him?'

The younger one went in and a minute later the doctor marched out.

'Hey. What's this Anne tells me? You think you can drive my horses, hey? They're the finest in the county, my dear sir. The finest by far.'

I still insisted I could manage. He looked hard at me, then walked to one side and stared, then he walked behind and had a long survey. Why this was I never learned but it took a couple of minutes then he decided:

'Ah well. I wash my hands of it. You hear, Helen, and you Anne? I wash my hands. Call me when you are ready.'

I went inside the stables, supported at a short distance by the two maids. Those stables were not on the same rugged lines as our stables at home. Rows of glass cases in the saddle room held several sets of highly polished harness. In the stables next door were three superb horses. One big chestnut with white fetlocks, a dapple grey and a coal-black horse, all with ears up and heads turned to consider what was happening. I picked a set of harness and fixed it on the chestnut without anything more unusual than a few swishes and squeals. During this time the maids had opened some double doors and with some panting and struggling had drawn out a light American gig. While they held the shafts, at the length of their arms, I got the prancing chestnut in place and quietly fastened traces and straps. The two girls were nervously coaxing the horse by rehearsing loving talk on him. Helen had warned me about the way the three horses had been spoiled for starting so I was most wary. With the reins lying slack on the brass rod I told my helpers to stand clear, put a foot on the step, grabbed the reins and tumbled into my seat in one lightning move.

Swift as I was it was not too hurried. At the sound of boot touching step the chestnut jumped forward and had I tightened the reins he would have leapt into the air. I just steered slackly and we swung round the corner of the saddle room and on to the main road with not more than an inch to spare. Then I let him go at his fastest and it was speed. Hoofs shining black, white fetlocks flashing, and front legs curving almost up to his nose, he was a magnificent sight. The rubber-tyred gig, with a tinkling bell on the front rail, was like a wicker basket behind him. A mile along there was a big curve around a playing green. He could just endure to be guided gently round and away we travelled back towards the surgery. Nearing the house I could see the doctor doing what seemed a Zulu dance near the double doors. I understood his signals to mean that I was to slacken but not try to stop. I knew it would be near fatal to force that plunging horse to stop anyway but I did ease up considerably and with the reins in one hand and both eyes on the doctor I prepared for the climax.

It seemed his feet wanted to get on the step but his instincts wanted to get back into the house. Finally, with agony showing on his face, he plunged forward, got a foot on the narrow step and stumbled up. As his head and shoulders came forward I grabbed at the velvet collar and dragged him to safety. He struggled into his seat, put the silk hat into proper position, then sat up trying to look as if he had control of the situation.

By the time we had reached near our home some of the steam had gone from our chestnut but there was always plenty of go in him. I kept moving at a gentle trot while he was with the old lady and the second stumble into the gig by the doctor was not so ungraceful.

'Your home is along the road, hey?' he asked.

'Stop for a minute there then,' he said when I had answered.

Again the gentle trot up and back and I went right down to the village and circled the preaching cross so that any friends who might be watching should see my style. Then I heard something like a police whistle sounding near my home and trotted more swiftly to see what was the noise about. It was the doctor's signal that he was ready. My mother was at the bottom of the garden holding a case which she pushed into the gig.

'The doctor wants you to help him for a week or so until he gets another married man,' my mother explained while the doctor stood erect alongside. As the chestnut started to prance he lifted his silk hat gracefully then scrambled in beside me and we were off. We made a couple of calls on the way and returned to the surgery. As we swung round the saddle room I saw we had almost a reception committee. It was as if we had been out with a lifeboat. The doctor's wife was there. I felt she was younger than he was and she was still slim and nice-looking. There was a trio alongside her. Each dressed in black dress, black stockings, stiff white apron and tiny lace cap. The four were exactly the same height, about five foot six. Helen was dark-haired, Anne fair-haired, and Lucy was a redhead. The gig creaked, and the doctor dismounted. The chestnut stood panting.

'Old Coombes does very well, now I've shown him the ropes.' he explained. 'And . . . oh Annie. Get a room ready for old Coombes. He's staying for a week or so. We want our lunch too . . . at once.'

So for him always I became 'old Coombes'. I was about a week short of sixteen and he was sixty-five.[3] That week lasted almost a year and would have been indefinite had I not been so eager to see more of the world. I did not guess it then but I had finished with farm work in that area for ever except for a few days at holiday time. No more walking across the quarter-mile long fields behind the plodding shires.[4] No more sweating in the corn harvest or keeping the tally in the hop yards. Usually my father could manage all the work at our small farm and I went to work at the Castle which had about six hundred acres of plough land.[5] I had been doing a man's work there and carrying a man's load. I had liked the work and the life but somewhere Destiny moved a switch and I was almost a gentleman.

In the afternoon we had a similar adventure with the grey and by then I had my uniform on. Kid gloves, bowler hat, and a white mackintosh coat which was a magnificent garment. I have never found another like it. Often I sat for hours in teeming rain and not one spot penetrated. How I hated that bowler and the gloves. In other ways my life had changed also. An only child, brought up to

---

[3] This would date the episode as just after New Year 1909.
[4] Shire horses.
[5] Castle Farm, Madley.

work every hour of every day, I was now surrounded by young femininity. In the country at that time there was little chance of excitement, so in the evenings we used to play whist in the kitchen while the doctor and his wife sometimes had musical evenings in their front section of the house. The doctor played at the violin while his wife was an excellent pianist. The vicar used to come once or twice a week with a flute. They certainly did not make great music but even their efforts brightened the evenings and caused me to find a love of music which developed in my life into orchestral playing.

Helen was from Ammanford and had a lovely contralto voice. If the others went out on an evening she would have a spell in the front, singing and accompanying herself whilst I kept watch that the doctor or his wife did not return. Helen had been married to a man from that part but not happily and her husband had been killed by a horse in the first year of marriage. At twenty she was a widow, very attractive, and longing intensely to return to Wales.

Annie, the blonde, was about eighteen and full of the worries of love. She was courting, but not enthusiastically. When I had been there a few weeks and we were all on gossipy terms she unloaded her troubles on me. Fred, her present sweetheart, was about eight years older and he was well over six foot. To make up for that height he had sacrificed in width. Annie did not enjoy being squired by a long, weak-seeming man. I listened sympathetically.

'Yes,' Annie explained, 'I like courting . . . but I'm tired of Fred. I wish I could find someone different.'

'Like what do you mean. What sort of a chap?' I asked.

'Someone younger . . . and strong like. Just like you,' Annie explained.

I pondered over that, trying to think of someone I knew who would comfort Annie. I was good friends with her and wanted to help. It has since occurred to me that I was very slow in the uptake in those days for it often seemed that Helen was not averse to trying again some of the joys of marriage, and Lucy teased me continually. Still on the shy side I never realised the mystery of womanly ways. I was a bit elevated by that mention of strength from Annie and got more than usually rough with the young blacksmith at our nightly sparring in the shoeing shed. I drove round for a week with a black eye. He had one also but he could hide his more easily.

During the months I was there we travelled daily, and often nightly, along the roads outside Hereford and up the Golden Valley. I have since been astonished by the lack of interest I had in those places where history was sleeping. Kilpeck, St Devereaux, Ewyas Harold and Peterchurch were all steeped in the romances and tragedies of the past. Now I would have looked at every stone but then I drove past seeing nothing of them and only concerned with the urge to hasten the months along so that I would be a man in age.

How slowly the months crawl for youth. A year seems an age in passing but after middle age the years gallop as swiftly as we did during the months behind the high steppers. Once every week we went, usually by night, to the Workhouse at Abbeydore. We never put the horse inside there, so I trotted whichever it was quietly back and fore along the road, waiting for the whistle. Deep in thought, with only the carriage lamps lightening the darkness all around, I might be watching the shining harness or moving limbs of the horse when a voice would bring me sharply back to reality.

'Hey! Can you please tell us the way to the Union.'

It was a lonely place and they must have travelled quite a way even after finding the place where the ticket was granted. Whenever there was no danger of the doctor knowing, I got the 'milestone inspectors' up in the gig and several of them arrived at the Workhouse gates in fine style . . . in a polished gig and drawn by blood horses. I had secret talks with some regular inmates and took them a present of tobacco once a month. This was a joint present between the three girls and myself. The doctor made a great function of paying us in turn. That night we had a quiet beano. I bought the bottles of lemonade and some sweets and that was our jollification for that month. During the winter there were a couple of dances in a large room above the stables at a public house opposite. Some of them came for miles through snow or rain to dance to the music of a violin, piano and drums.

One bitter night I walked the horse and gig around a large meadow from midnight until seven the next morning. It was a very isolated home. The man was a forester and at some time in the night he brought me out a cup of tea but forgot milk. Hours later he brought another – no sugar that time. I expect the worry of his wife upset him but the baby came all right and at daybreak, with the gig partly full of snow, we started homewards.

'Anne, Anne, quick now,' he called, 'I want my breakfast and old Coombes wants his too. We've been at the North Pole all night.'

He came to call me at once while we were having lunch and was astounded that he could see no glass of beer. I said I was a teetotaller.

'Teetotaller? Fiddlesticks. Look around at those pasty-faced cranks and then look at me. Anne! See that old Coombes drinks a glass of beer every day.' So there was one less teetotaller.

Some of the outlying farms made their own beer and great stuff it was. They had also a selection of wines, their own bread, butter, cheese, mutton and bacon. They had, as we had at home, the brick oven built into a wall and big enough to hold a week's baking and cooking for a large household. What a grand smell of fresh bread and cakes came to greet us when we called at such places. There was no getting away until we also had fed. Sometimes a call about illness would lead to the horse being stabled and our visit lasting into the night. I had some stupendous meals at several of the farms and, despite my eager health, did not feel really hungry for days afterwards. At a couple of the very rich patients I had supper in the servant's hall while the doctor was somewhere else. Always the habit then was for bare tables with the boards scrubbed white and stone or tiled floors. One place had sixteen servants, all but two female. They were all with me at supper and I was too embarrassed to enjoy the mild jokes of the butler at the far end of the table. A small slice of stale cake and two pieces of bread which had been lightly kissed by something akin to butter was my share. That appeared to be the normal menu and every ounce of food had to be accounted for by the housekeeper.

When later I found one of their grooms admiring my horse in their stables I told him of my disgust at the meal. Most of the girls either had food sent to them or went starving, he said. 'But the family does themselves very well.'

If he took a parcel to the station and it cost sixpence to send he had to hand a receipt from the station in when he returned. Needing netting wire for a short length of fence they had a roll from the ironmongers, used those few yards then sent the rest back and only paid for what they had used. New brushes bought for distempering were washed and returned to the shop when the work was done. When I said this was something new to me he said: 'I know. But that's how they comes and stays as millionaires, see?' So now you know.

One job I used to detest. About every fortnight a large basket container had to be fetched the mile from the station. It contained new medicine bottles and drugs. Because of the risk of running away or getting smashed he would not allow me to fetch it with any of our horses or the gig. The only alternative I ever saw was a donkey and cart. If I could not avoid fetching that load myself I was savage for hours before and after. There were houses all the way and I felt that each housewife had a grin on her face as I passed. My starting off with the girls sharpening their wit was bad enough, but at the station it nearly always threatened battle between the porters and myself. If we were fairly busy however I escaped and the local tailor did the job. He had only one leg and folks could not very well laugh at him. He was desperately poor but always he had a 'dead snip', for the next day's racing. As he often had to borrow a shilling or two off me and had several children I felt his snips were more dead than successful. As I remember him he used to make complete suits for the farmers.

I had been warned one night not to go far away as the doctor was expecting a call. He would not walk a hundred yards. It was a cold night and I considered the situation by the warm stove in the saddle room. I decided that I was entitled to smoke in my waiting time. Besides that I had a desire to spread a rich, scented smell all around. Amongst a mixture of many things the chemist sold tobacco and I conferred with him over the problem. I decided to start with cigarettes and as no firm seemed to make suitably rich-smelling ones – I do not recall why neither of us thought of cigars – I came away with two packets of cigarette papers and two whole ounces of Royal Seal tobacco. That was to provide the seductive smell. I have thought it strange since then that although I was quite indifferent to comfort and pretty tough in most things I loved the smell of good perfume. To that end I was going to make my own in a manly way.

The cigarette shaping was not a success. I could not roll them correctly. Over to the chemist's again for a consultation. Obviously a pipe was the only hope. Three and sixpence was quite a price then but after all, as the chemist explained, I was young and would be smoking for many years.

That really did go better. I filled the pipe, reduced its contents to ashes and filled it again. When that was ashes I tried to locate the warm, comfortable smell which seemed to result from other men's efforts but could not detect any. Possibly the pipe had not matured so I filled and smoked it busily twice more. I know now that one can hardly notice his own smoke smell but I was disappointed and worried that I could not detect an aroma around the stables. It was becoming rather late by that time and something strange was happening to the stables. The horses and walls were dancing around me. I stumbled out to the side and a shrub which I had trimmed very neatly the week before took on all sorts of shapes and actually moved about. I went back into the saddle room and sat down, unable to move.

As I had not answered the call to supper Helen came to hurry me up. I did not want supper. I felt more like dying. Helen sniffed and noticed the pipe and tobacco. I could not have moved to hide them in any event. She sniffed and said:

'Oh, that's the game, is it? I suppose you're like us women at a certain time. You'll have to be worse before you get better. I'll put your supper in the oven.'

She brought the other two out to view me in my misery then I sat alone in a hard, vibrating world until near midnight then crept to bed. I woke early next morning and went on with the routine jobs. I had mainly recovered from the experiment.

About eight o'clock a miserable figure shambled past the double doors and came hopefully towards me. I was considering the hardness of life at sixteen. He had slept rough on that bitter night. Did I think they would give him a bit of food? He motioned towards the house, inside which the maids could be seen moving about. 'Sure, I said, I'll go and persuade them.' I brought him out a plate of ham sandwiches and a mug of tea. He warmed himself at the stove and ate greedily. Then he stood up.

'Thanks laddie,' he said, 'I feel a lot better now.'

He started to walk away, then I had an idea.

'Do you smoke?' I asked.

He smiled wistfully, as if at some long lost pleasure. He nodded and still moved away. I hurried after him and into a hand which was shaking with surprise I pushed a new pipe, almost two ounces of tobacco, the cigarette papers and matches. He looked as if dazed for a minute, then thanked me quietly, stuffed the tobacco in expertly, lit up and marched away. He waved to me as he came to the turn and do you know, I felt very warm and comfortable over it but he it was who was dispersing that luxuriant smell.

Satisfied with my defeat I did not try to smoke again for more than twenty years. I was more successful next time but it never enslaved me.

~

Every morning there sounded a slippered scuffling along the main passage, a storm of spluttering and coughing out by the garden, and the doctor had 'cleared himself out' for another day. Things were more leisurely on a Sunday morning but now and again Lucy came across with the whispered warning:

'They've had a row. They're not speaking, so look out.'

They all knew the drill. Just before the doctor's wife would start for the walk along the road to the chapel, which was about a hundred yards away, the doctor would come dashing out at much greater speed than he showed even on an urgent call. He had on his gardening uniform – slippers, a faded dressing gown and a smoking cap.

'Old Coombes. Old Coombes . . . Annie . . . Helen . . . Where the devil is she? . . . Oh there you are. Quick. Bring the . . . the thingumbobs that they use in the garden out there at once.'

The garden was placed high, and in full view from the road. His wife marched past, stiffly erect, and the minister, deacons and most of the congregation did the same. If anyone happened to greet us the doctor leaned grandly on whatever tool he was misusing at the moment and wiped away imaginary sweat. When the road was empty and the organ tunes, played by his wife, sounded out to us the doctor ceased any vague effort he was making.

'Well that's that. It looks a bit better, hey? Think we deserve a little rest now. I'm not so young as I used to be.' The incident was closed.

Most of the outlying farms had dogs and also the cottages. They were often necessary guards. The doctor had no liking for dogs. He had told me about one early morning call as a young man when he answered a call, and getting no reply to his knock, opened the door and was immediately knocked down and bitten by a big dog.

'Took great pieces out of me, it did. Most horrible feeling I ever had, I assure you. Wouldn't have been much of me left if help had not come.'

Looking at his massive figure I thought there would have been one dog who had found enough to eat if that had happened.

When I recounted that affair at tea one evening Annie said she had heard of a man being a 'dog's dinner' but never being a 'dog's breakfast'. Anyway, ever since, his danger radius away from dogs was an extensive one. Most of the cottage dogs were tethered and their chain left room to pass if one went reasonably, but not the doctor. Naturally the dog would bark, the doctor, umbrella at the ready, would then advance very stealthily. If the dog did not retreat the doctor would jab with the umbrella.

'Bite at me would you? I'll teach you. Hear him. Not safe to be about.'

When the dog got really nasty he would retreat towards the gate and start blowing that powerful whistle that he used to warn all other traffic that we wanted a clear road. Then he would refuse to go to the house until the dog was shifted and not tied near the door whenever he called.

Motor cars were beginning to upset his way of life by the noise and smell they caused on the roads. Often in those days they broke down and he always touched my arm if he saw one disabled so that he could gloat as we passed.

'Silly old things, you know. Nasty smelly things. Never do any good with them.'

Yet he thought it wise to learn just a little about them in case he had to use one some day. So he bought the few publications which dealt with them and the gig was always littered with them.

'Ah yes. You had better study them while I'm making the house calls. You never know. If I did decide to have one, very improbable you know, if I did have one would you learn to drive it?'

That would then have been a great delight and I said so. He looked somewhat suspiciously at me and we left it at that. One result did show plainly for no longer were we the fastest vehicle on those roads. The honking horn was challenging his whistle.

One dark night we were trotting quite amicably towards Long-town. As we started to go up the slope from a deep hollow we heard a rushing sound and two bright lights appeared above us. It looked and sounded to the doctor, no doubt, like a monster with two glaring eyes and a roaring breath. It was the first time I had met such a danger by night. The horse did not like it either. I realised it was the motor car bought by a millionaire racing stable owner who lived not far away. Even in those pioneer days they went for the biggest and noisiest. It was tricky controlling a dancing horse on that narrow road but we passed safely. I wondered why the doctor had been so silent and after the lights had passed I turned to speak. He was not there. At the sight of that advancing terror he had jumped for it and had landed head first in a thick blackthorn hedge. I expect you have never tried to drag a sixteen-stone man out from a hedge which was not willing to let him go and hold a powerful horse which was as much frightened as the man at the same time. I can assure you it is rather difficult. Finally I did it, and also rescued the silk hat with only a few scratches on it. I helped him back into the gig and we went sadly on our way.

Mounting and handling the horses was much easier by that time. They were still very fast and lively but had lost their fear of being handled. We were friends now and I could walk around the orchard on a summer's night and the three would walk sedately behind me, much to the delight of the girls. It had all been a question of very bad handling. Nervous men jerking at the reins, twisting and hurting their mouths, and beating them in the stable for any little liveliness. Before myself the doctor had unwittingly followed the colliery and army method. If you have a job put someone to do it who should be doing something else. Hardly ever are country men used as hauliers in the mines. Instead, men with no knowledge or sympathy are used. I know there is a difference in the work but the nature of a horse is the same and more than ten thousands are still used in our mines in this year of 1959. Do not let anyone persuade you that the underground is an Eldorado for horses, although their treatment has improved during recent years. Of course I never drove regularly underground and was either working the coal or on maintenance work. I drove horses only in emergencies. Similarly at Aldershot. I had a great deal of ambulance experience, and was an expert rider. Just the chap for the RAMC or possibly a mounted section. Not so – I was made a clerk for a while at any rate. Then, when I had mastered that, I was transferred to the wards.

This doctor was quite fond of a stimulant which it seems that many more doctors feel is much better than the ordinary medicine. On a quiet night he would get across to the public house which was fairly close. With a couple of the other main characters in that village he was placed nicely from sight and interruption in the kitchen. If a call came one of the maids would take the message over. He would come to the door and ask particulars. If it was someone he knew he would come reluctantly and I would have to go with him for whatever the time and the weather he would not walk. Also even a short journey meant that horse and harness had to be cleaned again. Sometimes it would be a labourer in a distant cottage or a tramp found in a ditch. When he had that news the result was different.

'Ha. Right out all that way hey? Let them get another doctor. Tell old Coombes to tell 'em the usual.'

'The usual' was that the horse was lame or the harness broken. While the messenger was going away through the night I could look at three horses in fine fettle scrunching their oats or sit alongside eight sets of polished harness in glass cases.

If we had a busy period clipping was rather complicated. As he needed it badly I started on the chestnut after supper one night with the intention of working into the morning to finish him. After half past eleven an urgent call came. The other two had done very long journeys that day so I had to take the chestnut. He was only half clipped and I was on the point of starting the other side when the call came. We went through the night with one side of the horse showing a dark chestnut and the other much lighter. I noticed the doctor looking rather unbelievingly at our horse once or twice but possibly he thought it was the lamplight, or his eyes. He never said anything and I never told him.

Late one wintry night we were called to a large mansion about a mile away. A carter on the Home Farm belonging to that mansion had been giving the last feed to his charges when he found two men and two young women asking for some place to spend the night. They had failed to get in anywhere else. He put them amongst the sweet smelling hay in the loft. It was a modern repetition of the Nativity story. I think the resemblance appealed to the doctor for he astonished many by the way he acted afterwards.

That night one of the young women had a baby. We were called and the child was all right. I expected the woman to be sent to the workhouse which was about three miles away and they had been tramping. Suddenly the doctor surprised everyone and made an enemy for life of the titled owner. That mother and child had to be taken into the mansion and kept there until he felt it safe to move her. Useless for the owner or his wife to argue. The doctor was adamant and into the house they were carried and he saw they were put into a good bedroom. What a commotion there was. The wealthy owner stormed at the doctor and his abuse was returned in full. The owner got his revenge by going out and sacking the carter on the spot. Parading back and fore along the wide drive I watched the scurrying about of the female staff. They were all flustered and not adequately dressed. I meditated quietly on the terms I had heard the doctor and the owner use to each other. College had not made them very proficient at swearing, I felt, but their meaning was fairly plain. We drove there every day for a fortnight and not even the footman met the doctor at the door. After that fortnight the place was forbidden ground to us and we never again went there. The doctor was quite a local hero after that and every one touched their forelocks to him, a salute which he gravely accepted. The carter was moved into the cottage which went with my job and was found work at a cider factory which was newly started. The doctor appeared to have forgotten completely that it might be needed for a groom. He however needed my opinion about the happening over the baby.

'Did the only decent thing, you know. A fellow has to have a little human feeling, hey. What do you say, old Coombes?'

The autumn came and the garden ditches and the orchard had to be cleared out. He engaged the two local odd-job men to do that. It meant a day's work and he paid them by the hour. So he cancelled the rounds for that day, put on a thick overcoat, polished his glasses, filled his tobacco pouch and made me carry an easy chair into the garden. There he sat with the watch in his hand, one eye on the watch and the other on the workers.

That did not suit their ideas at all. If they paused ever so slightly he gave a warning cough. After a couple of hours they were about exhausted. I busied myself about the stables but when they were near the limit I went past them in the garden.

'That old bugger will kill us,' one whispered, 'can't you get rid of him somehow?'

'I'll shift him.' I promised. I had been asked to kill a young cockerel so I went into the cot, caught him, and marched up to the doctor. I opened my pocket knife as I got near and I could see the alarm spreading over his features. I knew his weakness.

'Is this the one you wanted killed, doctor?' I asked. He glanced quickly at the bird and the knife, got up clumsily, said 'Yes, I think so' and disappeared indoors. I killed and feathered the bird. Usually that took me about twenty minutes. The workers used that period well, they sat on their heels enjoying a cigarette. Leaving the dressed bird hanging in the coach house I went into the kitchen to look for Helen. She was the cook but only Lucy was there.

'What did you do to him?', she motioned towards the front section.

'Only ask him about the cockerel,' I said. 'Why?'

'He rushed in past here like as if the place was on fire, drank a glass of whisky, and dropped into a chair. The missus asked what was the matter and he said: "Good God. That old Coombes have got a nerve." '

He had several elderly and constant patients who lived at distant farms. We usually visited them once a week, or if he was not well I rode there with medicines. It seemed they did not pay him in cash but as winter came on waggon loads of hay, and straw, arrived daily. I was in my element. I made them into tidy ricks after the loft was full, and when they settled I thatched them so neatly that even the experts who watched from the roadside could do nothing but admire. Then came some sacks of oats and a couple of waggons laden with logs. I had to saw these into blocks and this task, which I did easily, had been counted as very hard by the previous grooms. The doctor, all the while our farming was happening, had stood with hands in pockets at a safe distance. When all was neat and swept up he threw his shoulders back and said:

'We have made a good job of that, old Coombes. A very neat job. Think we deserve a rest now.'

Later a truck load of coal was carted from the station and as it was delivered, I put it in. When it was all under cover he was content.

'Now we're right for the winter. Come on in. Helen . . . a large glass of beer for me and for old Coombes. We've been working hard.'

Helen brought it. She was smiling, and she was very nice to look at. We drank our beer, and I turned to go out. The doctor was in the passage when he said:

'Yes. We're right now. I don't care if those old miners strike now.'

I knew it was only a laboured joke on his part but it hurt Helen like a kick. A strained whiteness chased the smile from her face and I left her standing, gripping the table. Later, I found her in the saddle room, so that the others should not see her tears. I tried to say it was a joke. She would not listen.

'The fat creature,' she spluttered, 'he's never done a real day's work in his life. One day in the mine would kill him. My father and brothers risk their lives for the coal to keep his sort warm. My uncle was killed in the pit. He shan't belittle them. I'm going back.'

They all tried to alter her decision but she was determined. She was a wonderfully good girl and they all knew it but all arguments were wasted. She gave notice and at the end of the month she went. Those weeks did not hurry enough for her. Each night she came for a period into the saddle room, hummed some of the well loved airs, and talked of Ammanford and its valley in that soft accented voice.

As Helen showed us and as I saw for myself later the miners' wives are supremely loyal to their husbands' work and so are all their womenfolk. You can usually find fault with them in various ways but do not ever say anything against them as a body of workmen. If they are on strike their womenfolk support them all the time and all the way. That is one consolation for no one class of people have been so misreported and slandered as the mining community. The strangeness of their work may have something to do with this but the big weakness is the poverty of the propaganda put out by the miners' union. All through the years they do not seem to have the least idea of how to explain their industry and its special difficulties.

I could rarely get an hour or two off to cycle across to my home, and the body which had been prepared to fight with a man if he tried to carry one more sack of wheat than me was getting slack in this comparatively easy job, so soon after Helen went I also departed. I was almost seventeen and wanted to shape the world up a bit. The doctor regaled me with tales of what bad things would happen to me if I went underground but his warning only made me the more eager. The hint of danger calls somehow to youth. When the last night came he was very downcast and dubious about the new man, middle-aged, who was coming. He gave me two pounds extra as a parting present explaining he had meant to buy me a watch but had not been to town. Perhaps I would buy the watch myself, he suggested.

I did not. I left the kid gloves, the bowler hat, and the driving coat in their place in the saddle room when I went. Thinking over it now, more than forty years later, I realise I have never had a watch in my life or a bowler hat or kid gloves since that day. I have never missed them but often I would have liked to have a coat so good as that one on a stormy day.

The doctor had a brother in Cardiff who wanted me to go to him. Helen had left her address and a promise of good care and lodgings. Relatives in Maerdy offered me the same and so did relatives in Treharris near whom I had lived before. Also there was a friend, older than myself, who had a place for me with him in the Vale of Neath. I solved this problem by putting slips in the bowler, after I had worn it for the last time, and assuring myself doggedly that whichever place I drew out, there I would go. The Vale of Neath won. Although tempted, I kept my solemn promise to myself.

Chapter Three

~

SUCH sudden and unexpected things alter your whole outlook on life. Up till that time I had thought only of working as hard and often as possible so that we could get that little farm which we thought would be our Shangri La. Now our savings were gone and with a poor chance of overtime or high wages we had to start again.[1] Then other complications came.

With one of my mates in the pit we were about to have food and had chosen a sheltered spot where the roof looked safe. My mate had actually opened his food tin when the deputy came urging us to come at once to clear a fall on the main roadway. It was so urgent that we went at once. My mate closed the tin, placed it back in his jacket pocket hung on the side, and said:

'I'll enjoy that grub later.'

To analyse it fairly I suppose no one could be really blamed. It was one of the events which occur every day in mining somewhere. The deputy had to get the rails clear so that coal could pass along. We had to go and work in what we saw was danger because work was scarce and we had dependants.

Ten minutes later I was standing dazed in complete darkness and silence. Each side of me, so close that I could touch either by spreading my elbows, was a huge stone which had fallen without a crack of warning from a height of about eighteen feet. In the darkness I called to the two men who had been with me. Neither could answer. I had seen many smaller accidents but this was the first time death had crashed down against my elbow. In that petrified minute before I crawled through the darkness to bring

[1] This suggests that the episode which Coombes goes on to describe occurred either after the stoppage of 1921 or that of 1926.

help which was of no avail, I realised how puny were even strong men.

I realised something else later. I was the only witness at the inquest. I realised that neither coroner, solicitors, or hardly any one present had the least idea of what happens under the earth. I also realised that to say that we protested against going there might give a loophole to the compensation companies. It might be argued that we should have refused, and the dependants of my mates might suffer. So I said just what was needed. They made it accidental death.

Inside me somewhere was the determination that I must do something to let the world know more about our way of life. I pondered long over it, lonely in my idea, but I never forsook the intention. Months later I started to write, with a copy book and pencil. I have skipped over that mining accident because it was written up as a long story and published by John Lehmann who afterwards became a very good friend. It was also done as a radio feature so I do not need to repeat it.[2]

Even from tragedy sometimes a laugh is born. I started work straight after the accident because it is best not to let the nerves dwell on fear. The atmosphere of a tragedy in the mine is very frightening. You have to work near the spot where you saw it happen and feel that all around are dangers waiting to crush you. That is unless the management is humane enough to move you to another section. They did not move me, and the next night I was working to complete the packing up of the roof and sides from which the fall had come. The afternoon shift had done some of it. It is difficult for one man to work alone in those conditions, and I believe it is against the Mines Act so they sent a new mate with me, a man who had been working as a labourer. He was from another district, not at all bright, and did not know what had happened at the exact place where we were working. His main assistance was as company and even at that he stood behind me

---

[2] Coombes is referring here to the short story 'Twenty Tons of Coal', published first in *New Writing* (New Series, No.3, Christmas 1939). Similar events are treated in Chapter Thirteen of *These Poor Hands*, and in 'A Miner's Record – III', *New Writing and Daylight* (Summer 1943). We have not been able to find any trace of its appearance as a 'radio feature'.

when I was pulling a stone down. I jumped back to save myself, banged into him, and so knocked the breath out of him and the light from his safety lamp. We all had oil lamps at that time.

He was a stranger there so he did not know where to find the relighter. I had to go back and take my lamp with me. I put this new mate safely in a refuge hole which was right by where we were working and told him not to venture out. As he had no light it would have been silly in any case. I had not told him about the accident and left him there chewing his tobacco. About sixty yards farther up was an old heading into which they were taking stone rubbish and another labourer, Will, was unloading a tram in there. I saw the faintest reflection of his light as I passed. He was hidden by a thick hanging of brattice cloth, tarred cloth, which hangs heavily and prevents the air from leaking.

Nat, my new mate, must have been near dozing when I had passed well out of sight. Some short time later the overman ambled along that way from lower down. As with most of us he felt a bit subdued near the fatal spot but wanted to see how the repairing was getting along. It was solid dark all around and he must have wondered where I had got to. He lifted his lamp to look upwards and to see if any gas was present. At that moment, Nat, in his dark manhole, saw that someone was about.

'Hoi there,' Nat spoke slowly always, in a sad voice. To the overman it must have seemed like a voice from the grave. He jumped, shrieked, and dropped his lamp. So he also was in the dark. Nat, now properly awake, heard a shriek and a crash below him, yet when he looked he could see nothing. Discretion urged him to scramble up the dark roadway to that distant shade of light that showed where Will was shovelling. His scrambling alarmed the overman who had no idea any living soul was there and in the darkness each could hear the other grunting and fumbling. I think Nat reached the brattice cloth first but could not find his way between the sheets. His desperate fumbling was hastened by the knowledge that something unknown was close behind him. Will heard the scuffling, and he knew about the accident. He turned fearfully and saw a hand, only a hand, thrust between the hanging sheets of tarred cloth. That hand was trying hard to grasp something so·that the rest of Nat could get through but Will thought it was something supernatural trying to get him. He was paralysed with terror and backed into the road until he could go no farther. Then he watched in terror as the two frightened men struggled desperately to get past the toils of that hindering cloth, neither knowing what this other body was, until at last both tumbled breathlessly through and the faint light of Will's lamp cleared up the mystery and gave them a chance to cool their nerves and regain their breath. When I got back with the lamps they were partly recovered and almost able to laugh at the fright. It is possible to smile afterwards but in darkness and with taut nerves things are not so amusing.

At one time I worked in a seam no more than eighteen inches high. Every morning I used to end, look under where the coal seam waited, and wonder how could I squeeze my body into that space, let alone do work in there. We lay on our sides and slid the coal back past our bodies. We moved about like swimmers and all the coal had to be blown out of that seam. One day a pocket of gas caught as I was charging a hole with dynamite. So low was the roof that I could not get up to run. I could have got away no quicker than a slow swimmer so I lay tight to the ground and hoped. The flash of gas flickered past the detonator, and the dynamite, but for some marvellous reason no explosion happened.[3]

Another time I went to connect the firing cable to a top hole I was firing. The shotsman went into a side road to prepare. He saw a light passing up and assumed it must be me as he had not been told of a stranger starting behind me that day. With a full pound of dynamite in the hole and me facing it as I connected the wires he tried three times to fire. Each time must have been before I made the wires completely connected. When I walked back to him he said it must be a flat shot. He tried once more then and it went off. A tighter twist to those two thin wires and I should have ceased to exist.

Mates working on the afternoon shift had charged a shot hole which had failed to act and dislodge the coal. With a young boy with me I started energetically next morning to chip under the coal. My mandrel was sharp and I was fresh. As I slammed into the hard coal the mandrel suddenly went in easily, and as I pulled back it had something fixed on the point and wires hanging. That

[3] This episode Coombes converted into his first published short story 'The Flame', *New Writing* 3 (Spring 1937), and also drew on it in *Miners Day* (1945).

was a couple of pills of dynamite and the detonator included. My mandrel point had passed the detonator by the merest fraction.

Working in one seam which was about twenty-two inches thick I was driving a coal-cutting machine which was about twenty inches high, thirty inches wide, and about ten foot long when the cutting jib was out. Quite a filler up in that small space. As I needed to pass by on one shift and there was no room on the side, I climbed and lay on top when we came to a part where a fallen layer had left a little more space. I thought to slide off behind but a screw nut caught in my waistcoat and I could not do so. The only other mate anywhere near had gone off to look for timber. I could not see his light and I had fixed the controls so that the machine would continue to pull ahead at half speed. In one more minute it would have dragged me under that lower roof and my body would have been squeezed through a space of two inches. I think that was the most terrible minute I ever had. A miracle saved me. The sledge slid from my hand, dropped on the revolving picks, they cut the handle away like slicing a piece of butter, and the sledge bounced up, hit the roof, dropped again on the circling picks and locked them as they caught against the solid coal. The strain caused the fuses to blow. The machine stopped and I lay for a couple of minutes shivering with fright.[4]

Walking along a main heading one day I slung my sledge and shovel over my shoulder like a rifle as I hurried. A large stone dropped from about fifteen feet, as big a stone as I could roll, and caught the shovel, knocking it from my grasp.

At one colliery where we used to ride in for a long distance in a journey of empty trams six middle-aged men always sat together, three-a-side, in their tram. That was the usual custom. We would argue, or banter, on that slow ride inwards. One day they pulled in about two hundred yards past the mouth and the rope stopped. An inquiry was shouted in for two of these six men. They had done something wrong and the overman wanted to see them outside. They grumbled about the delay which meant we would go on and they would have to walk. We did move on for about another two hundred yards. Without a crack of warning the roof above that one tram where the remaining four sat, collapsed, and

---

[4] This was 'fictionalized' as 'Machine Man', *New Writing* 5 (Spring 1938), and also appeared in *These Poor Hands* (1939).

filled the tram like one fills a square packet with sand. The maddening part was that steel arches and timber made a solid barrier each side of that one tram and all the strength which could find room to lift could not move one piece. We dared not try to move the ropes even had the engine been able to. It might have done some damage to the men as we could not find out their condition. All of us were far from the working places where the tools were but finally they were brought after a desperate rush and we started to clear the blockage. It was too late.

It stirred again a train of thought which has always intrigued me. Why do some escape throughout a life filled with danger while others do not? Is there some malignant fate trailing some? Why were those two called away, and that sole tram the only one on which the fall came? That one mate who worked with me and was killed by that big fall – at the beginning of the week a fast journey of trams nearly caught him and I only just managed to drag him into a refuge hole, on the Tuesday night a large timber collar dropped on him as he was passing underneath but we rolled it off without him suffering more than a bad bruising. On the Wednesday night he did not escape.

Dai Harris was a rope rider who sometimes drove a horse. One night the horse ran away and Dai escaped with a gashed leg. A couple of shifts later he was pulling trams of rubbish in to a trio of labourers in a stall road. The tram slipped off the rails and pinned Dai against the side but this was a quiet horse and he stood. We heard his gasp and went to help but two of us could not lift the heavy tram. We could see the labourers' lights, they were eating food and talking until the trams arrived. I shouted to them for help as Dai was getting crushed slowly. They did not seem to understand so I bawled again:

'Come on Erny. Give help – Dai is under a tram.'

Even then they could not have fully understood for the reply was a source of teasing for many days – 'I can't come, mun. We're having grub.'

A third, and more profane calling, stirred them up and with their added weight we freed Dai with only a few more sore places which did not stop him from being very sarcastic at the labourers' expense.

On the Friday night Dai was moving the journey of full trams. The engine driver had pulled them to the required place and the ten loaded trams waited, fast to the steel rope, for the other rope rider to take them back to the main engine house. There was little room on the side and Dai signalled that the engine was not to move the rope as he started to squeeze by. The well understood signal was a knock of ten on the signal wires and the engine driver would not move the rope again until that knock was cancelled. The driver felt like a drink and turned to where he had put his tea jack on a ledge. Dai was at the narrowest part then. As the driver swung round his lamp cable hooked under the control lever and lifted it. The engine jumped to full speed at once. When the driver jumped round and dropped the lever it was too late. It was the third and last time for Dai.

Why go on? It happens so often in that dark world where I was spending my working life. The general public either cannot understand or do not want to. A commercial traveller argues that he risks his life on the road in his car. He does, but miners use cars and buses, and walk the roads so they also have those risks. Since 1926 when I started with ambulance study I have had to treat these men, so often take their bodies home, and see the look on their wives' and children's faces. They were the men who had joked with me earlier in the shift. I knew their hopes, and I knew what treatment in compensation they might get.

Things end happier sometimes. One night we were busy working when some distance away we heard a terrific roar, and the roadway was so full of flying stones and dust that we had to retreat. About fifty yards farther down was the ambulance cabin where I kept stretchers and splints and the heavier things I needed. Another three repairers staggered in there with us, all white with dust and cut about the face from flying stones.

'She's gone up. We're lucky to be alive.' That was the idea while stones rattled against our closed door and a roaring sound continued outside. We settled down to await events. Only one lamp was left burning in case we were there for days. We moistened wide bandages ready for our mouths in case of foul air. When the roar quietened we ventured slowly out, to see if we could help some other survivors. A hundred yards farther towards the colliery mouth we found the trouble. A huge stone had fallen, cutting right through a pipe, as large as a man's body, which carried compressed air into the workings. That roar we heard was the air escaping before the engineer outside realised something was wrong and stopped the compressor. The power of that escaping air would lift a man off his feet and blew everything loose before it.

At one of the divides we had a curve and for a couple of weeks the big journey of trams never went round there without some leaving the rails and causing trouble. One night Bob and me were working half-way down the slope and we had a full tram of coal to act as a staging so that we could reach the steel arches on which we were placing packing. Bob was standing on this looking up at our problem when I went farther down to get a hatchet. I heard a crash and hurried back. A very long way back a shackle had broken and quite out of control eight loaded trams ran back at express speed. This time when it would have been better had they fouled the rails they kept the track perfectly and rushed down at our solitary tram where it was held by sprags and a rail against the side. There was a terrific crash. When I struggled through the dust it was almost a pile of scrap iron. Wheels had been torn off some trams, rubbish and coal was piled all around. I started desperately to search for Bob. MacCartney, the rider, arrived at the run to see what damage had occurred. Quietly, but desperately, we started moving things so as to find the body of my mate. As we were on our knees scraping a voice spoke from above us:

'Be careful, my watch is in my waistcoat somewhere there.'

Hearing the runaway coming he had swung himself up to safety above the steel arches and that cool action had saved his life. It was the only way to escape.

Chapter Eight

~

I WONDER can I explain what that morning meant to our lives and spirits? It was more than a decade ago and one can surely judge if the hopes and thrills have been justified. It was the morning when we came out from work and on the walk downwards to the baths we noticed that no day shift man had come up. It was a mild morning with the sun just peeping over the mountain and polishing the tops of the safety helmets worn by about a thousand miners who filled the road outside the baths so that the short ceremony should be watched.

Vesting Day, the first shift in our industry with the hopes of the past realised.[1] Throughout the land at that minute nearly three quarters of a million miners were attending similar ceremonies at their collieries. About thirty years since Bob Smillie, Frank Hodges and Herbert Smith produced such a case, and miners with their wives gave such convincing evidence, that Justice Sankey, one man who was not influenced by wealth, found that his trained mind could bring no other verdict than the condemnation of the methods used by the four thousand coal owners.[2] Their ownership had been blackened by misery for millions of decent people and it was time for it to end. That a man can be hanged for murdering one person yet be paid compensation if he has done that to the minds and bodies of hundreds seems a queer assessment of British justice. Also, even after the judge had given his verdict the years passed along before the sentence was taken to its

---

[1] Vesting Day was 1 January 1947.

[2] Robert Smillie, Frank Hodges and Herbert Smith were the nominees of the Mineworkers' Federation of Great Britain who sat on the Sankey Commission.

end. Miners and their wives who had been eager with youth when the Commission sat became weary and middle-aged as 1919 went farther and farther back into history. Some easements were given, pit-head baths and canteens were built, the seven-hour day was gained and taken away again, but the control was as harsh still as the mineral it worked.

I wonder does history give enough reward to the generation of workers who were the foundation of those years. They had indeed been forged in a testing time. Many of them going too young to a war and many being sent back as indispensable, then through years of slack work or complete unemployment until Germany revived again and they found that as soldiers, or as workers, miners were in great demand always during war time, but rarely at other periods.

May I give one of the many examples of how the mines were handled in those days? I offer this because the man concerned worked with me as a boy, then when he was eighteen went back to a colliery near his home at Aberdare. He was a finely-built youth and had boxed with success as a middleweight. One afternoon, months after he had gone back I went in to have a drink while waiting for a bus, and saw a back which I thought was familiar turned to me as I stood by the bar. I walked around to make sure and it was Latimer. Mutual delight and an extra drink followed. He had a suitcase with him and was selling cheap jewellery from door to door and doing well, so he said.

'Not in the pits?' I asked.

No more pit work for him, Latimer said and told me his last experience. After going to this fresh colliery he had been working as a collier. He was too young to claim the legal minimum wage but the result would have been the same in any event. He had worked hard, and been lucky to have a place where the coal was easy working. I think the price was two shillings and sixpence for a ton of large coal. He had managed, through youth and strength, to fill enough coal to earn the minimum wage and that had been paid. Also he had worked at clearing a fall and some other tasks which would have brought him another ten shillings or so, and that was a sum to value in those days. This extra had not been paid so the morning after pay day saw Latimer waiting outside the undermanager's office before going down the pit. There were about a dozen other men there – all seeking wages which had not been paid. Each went in to make his claim. Latimer stated what was missing and how it had been earned. The deputy was questioned and agreed the work had been done. All right, the undermanager wrote out a pay slip for that amount. All the men got their lamps and went down in their turn.

At the pit bottom was another deputy. He told Lat and the others to wait on one side. After the others had gone in bye he told the waiting men, all of whom had been after arrears of pay, that orders had come for them not to go on to work but to go back up the pit.[3] They had been allowed to descend then ordered back up. They had finished. There was no more work for them at that colliery. Latimer was not greatly worried. He was single, but that night the wife of one of the other men called at his home. They asked how she was faring. 'What could we do,' she asked, 'we got six children and we've got to live. I went to see the undermanager and after a bit he was willing for Tom to start back if he promised never to make a fuss about his money again.'

Latimer did not beg, he went to work for his sweetheart's father who was a jeweller and soon Latimer was married, so here he was, handsome and finely built, with the requirements for a good miner, walking round the doors with a small attaché case 'and better off, butty. You believe me, no more mining. Have another with me.'

Then the other men, what became of them? The pattern was well known and constant. They went to register at the Labour Exchange and by the time they arrived a telephone call had come from the colliery office asking for a dozen competent colliers. What about the men who have just registered, the unemployment manager might inquire. The reply would be that they were sacked for insubordination or because they were not trying. So they would have a penalty of six weeks' dole stopped. Another dozen men would have to go there to take their places well knowing that they would not get the minimum wage and would be treated in similar fashion. That way the married men were completely demoralised. Unable to get a fair wage they were sullen at work and savage at home. These methods destroyed men's happiness and broke their spirits. These methods did, however, produce a fairly large output of cheap coal, at a cost to human decency.

[3] 'In bye': towards the coal face.

When, later, the Coal Board looked for officials who had good records on paper, there they were.

We had an influx of these men during one slack period and the difference of mentality from the average village miner was astonishing. What I am calling villages usually contain from seven to eight thousand men with appropriate chapels and public houses. Often not more than a mile separates two such villages but each has its own limits. The miners there know each other well and know what problems the seams provide. They discuss them on the street corners or in the union meetings and are very loyal to each other. The old customs which have value are strictly guarded and even in bad times the men were politically conscious and kept their independence of spirit.

The invaders from larger and distant towns showed the effects of years during which they had not dared to answer back or claim what was due to them. Usually they were servile, not much interested in union rules or customs which did not give them an advantage. Very soon they lowered the working standards of the men amongst whom they worked. Before that we had insisted that each man had a complete set of tools and these were private for he had paid for them. It was not long before tools were stolen and broken. A stiff check on the new hands proved that they were using other men's tools and we acted sharply. We had tried to keep Sunday working to a minimum and had not been willing for coal to be filled on Sunday nights. Now we had men trying to break that rule and instances of men asking to come to work on Sunday for the payment of one shift instead of double time. Their excuse was that things were so dull on Sunday in their town. Possibly that was because the public houses were not open and a couple of them had been barred from entering the clubs. As one deputy stated pompously: 'These foreigners know our value. They say "sir" to us and the locals won't.'

One man worked near us for quite a while and was paid high wages. His special virtue, and he was proud of it, was that he kept a keen watch for any fresh woman that he could spot 'on the game' in any of the distant town public houses and so was able to act as guide for one overman on his Saturday night forays after 'skirt'. That overman was married with several children and a leader in the chapel. Admittedly he was a tactful person and knew how to handle men, and women apparently, and he treated the miners as well as he could.

We had another, with a brother working on the coal. He was not an expert collier and on the night shift was shuffled about to work in any stall where the coal was loose. This brought continual complaints from the men who worked those stalls. My mate and myself were on a fixed day-rate as repairers but every Friday night we had to do a good spell of cogging for part of the shift. This would have brought us about the value of our shift but as we well knew it was booked to the collier and made his into a very good pay. Of course ours was booked in as day work for us so we did not suffer and the overman wangled it somehow.

I recall complaining to another hard-bitten miner that this collier was working in an unsafe place and not placing any fresh timber for support. I got a rather inhuman assurance of:

'Don't you worry, bachgenny. Just keep that ambulance box handy. We'll hear him squealing just now.'

Another from that town came to work near us and he was not used to repairing either. Yet we found out he was getting a higher rate of pay than any of us who had been on the job for years. At that time so much in each pound earned was kept back for your doctor. It was understood that you chose the doctor. The new man came after me, as a committee man, one night with a complaint. He had nominated one doctor but the deductions were going to another. What could he do? I suggested he complain at the office first and if he had no satisfaction he should give the case to me and I would put it before the full committee.

I saw him a few nights later and he asked me not to take it any farther. Did they transfer the deductions to the proper doctor, I asked? No, he stated. Why not take it up and make them, I suggested? 'I've been nosing around,' he said, 'and if I makes a fuss they might give it to my proper doctor and then my wages would be dropped.' What was happening to him was similar to many who came from that distance. They were paid more than their value so that the doctor would gain on deductions. Why? Because he was a close relative of some in the highest positions at that colliery.

That repairer fancied himself as a singer. He had ambitions towards broadcasting. As I had done some thirty or more broadcasts he sought me out as a trainer and adviser. During a period when we were waiting for empty trams I fixed up a steel bar with a food tin fastened on top. With a shovel blade behind it to help the acoustics, his head bent near the tin and right hand cupping the sound he delighted the three labourers who were throwing rubbish into the waste pack. My training fee was a cup of tea in the canteen.

During the past years mining life had been lived under those shadows. My own father-in-law was without work for five years because of his union activity and he had been a checkweigher, elected by the men to watch that the company weigher did not fake the weight of trams coming out. These checkers were elected at every colliery and, believe me, they were needed. Also they were paid by the miners and were supposed to be completely outside the power of the colliery company. In many cases, however, they found a way of working even that elected representative out. It takes some courage to stand up for what you believe to be right even when it may hurt your wife and children and make yourself homeless and workless. As most villages had only one colliery it meant that to be blacklisted there was a sentence of idleness or banishment. Yet I knew, even in the bad times, many men, fine, sincere men, who would not do what they thought wrong even if it meant making an enemy of the management. In such a village the colliery manager then was the great Pooh Bah. I noticed there were usually three large houses in or near each mining village. In them lived the top trio – colliery manager, doctor, vicar.

Yet it was obvious that, even with the anchors dragging, the old ship of private enterprise was leaking at the seams and nearing its end. I have with me here the full report of the Sankey Commission. It is as heavy as a large lump of coal. It encloses the hurts and fears of an industry which had about three quarters of a million workers and their families. Families who bore the scars of a fatality oftener than once a day and an injury to one out of four every year. It was clear, however, that the conscience of the British public was stirring. Things had gone too far and too long.

~

One could sense the slackening during the last months before nationalisation was achieved. We could get things done in that period which had been refused bluntly earlier on. Our committee had asked for a spake for the night shift, and we tried to prove how the output would gain as all the men would be carried more swiftly to their working place and would not need to start out quite so early.[4] Also they saved the energy of that mile and a half walk underground. They would not consider it, yet just before Vesting Day it was started and went along nicely always afterwards. We had continually pestered that the night workers should be paid every Friday morning before they went home, but were told the idea was ridiculous. Night men had to go home and get a couple of hours sleep, get up, dress, and catch a bus again by about one o'clock then return home again for another attempt at sleeping. As many scores lived ten or twelve miles away Friday was a wearying day for them and it came right at the end of a week when many of them had not been able to get quiet during the day. This again was given us just before Vesting Day and was a great easement.

Then came that morning when we did not meet day men coming up the incline. They were massed on the road outside the pithead baths. A wintry sun peeped over the mountain to see what was going on as the announcement of Vesting was made. All over the land, at the same time, miners listened at nearly two thousand collieries. A new phase in our life had started. A great experiment in industry was to be tried out.

More than a decade has passed since those days and although mining must be an industry of slow progress it is time to consider the results. I feel most thinking miners will agree that we are very disappointed, and not a little ashamed of the stock-taking. It was an industrial adventure which had not been risked in this land before, and I felt that the unions and the workers should have ensured that it would sparkle with success: then other industries and other lands would have seen and copied. It seemed to come so unexpectedly, even after years of agitation, that neither men nor union were well prepared. I have been told that the plan was arranged by the Trade Union Council. Anyway, it was a plan that seemed to have no grip on what it sought to control. The miners and their union were like an army whose opponents have retreated but have no trained men ready to lead them in the new country and the fresh type of battle.

The Mineworkers' Union, knowing its aim, should have had hundreds of young men trained as deputies and in the higher branches of mining, men who believed in working to their limit for

[4] 'Spake': a carriage for conveying men underground in drift mines.

nationalisation. Any ordinary clear-thinking miner could pass the deputy's examination, the higher certificates need a sharper mind and longer study. I have often thought that no man should be counted a qualified miner unless he had passed the first mining examination. That would prevent a highly skilled and dangerous craft being looked upon by the ignorant as a refuge for all types. At one small colliery our undermanager had a mania for training men to pass as deputies. He spent all his spare time at it and guaranteed they could not fail. As he got eighty through out of four hundred working there I claim he knew what he promised. He had a big blackboard inside the ambulance room and one could seen the ½ × ¼ and so on where he had been teaching the middle-aged men how to do simple fractions and spell difficult words. Perhaps he was not so far off right in his ideas for even if the men had only a twenty-five per cent knowledge of book mining they had all the practical experience needed – and many of the present day officials' qualifications are of the reverse order.

That was a mountain colliery where we never had gas trouble, or much roof pressure, or any of the usual mining problems yet four men got first class manager's certificates while working there and they had never worked in any other colliery. Our union should have had a large number, anyway, of young men qualified, and ready to take over the mine controls. They did not have them and mining had to go on. As a result we changed the name over the shop which had failed and kept on the staff – that section which had caused most of the trouble. The men, even the lower officials, who had believed in the old control and done their best to make it continue were now handed the reins for nationalisation.

The companies who had driven their workers in the harshest way showed the best production figures. Because of their past records these managements were selected and often promoted under the new control. They were spiced with a few Army top brass who had outlived their usefulness and thought that a barrack-square manner was just the thing needed to terrify the miners and make them rush head first into the task of coal-getting. That infusion of marching mentality showed how far the Government was from understanding the minds of the miner. With the possible exception of a policeman no type will more surely annoy the independent miner than one who tries to impose a military atmosphere around him.

The miners' leaders, with all the country feeling they deserved better treatment, and at a time when coal was desperately needed, should have checked this sort of thing definitely and at once with the united power of its three quarters of a million members. Instead, they sat back, holding their bellies contentedly. Their sole concern was not to embarrass the Coal Board, and the couple of dear old pals who had been allowed to climb on the plush seats as a sop to the men, and themselves. I heard three miners' committee men talking last week. They had been interviewing the Coal Board about some point which had been refused:

'And who do you think were the worst swine against our arguments? Them two who used to be our leaders and was put comfortable by our votes and our union dues.'

Men who had been a joke even as deputies were put into much more responsible jobs. With appointment after appointment becoming known of men whose record made them hated or who had no mining experience the bright hopes of the miners started to fade.

Each pit had its working committee ready, and usually a consultative committee. They should have been made responsible for their own colliery. Close contact with the management should have been maintained with the management having the main voice in control. Each miner should have been paid the national rate for his job and a shared bonus for everyone employed given monthly if output figures warranted it. The output of different seams should be posted up on large boards and once a month the total output, with costs for working, prices for steel and timber and explosives. It should be possible for the committee to see what each miner had been paid, and each official. There should be a compulsory change of a section of the committee every year and the names of the firms from whom all supplies had been bought should be listed. A monthly meeting of all workers, with the management present, should be held and attendance made compulsory, against a fine.

Each group of collieries should have a joint committee and also a management board. There should be a flying team of three men on immediate call – like a rescue team, in case of any dispute developing. Both sides should have to abide by their decision and the dispute should be handled swiftly. One member of the disputes team should be from the miners, another from the management and the other independent but with a good knowledge of the industry. One or more of this team could appear without warning above or below ground at any colliery. Choosing the independent one would be the major difficulty.

~

Altogether it is a rather depressing tale of an ideal gone sour. The chance came in and the men should have been alert to scotch the opportunists. They should have had pride in their duty, in their industry and in their being chosen for such a great experiment. Men should have been at the head whom they would respect and there should have been no top or bottom dogs, just one great team. Maybe we will have to change our natures before such things can succeed. At present it looks that way.

~

I have been wondering how men who really wanted to make the coal industry democratic and humane would fare in these times with the humour of the men and control such as it is. I knew a couple of men who went from these areas to join the staff of the Coal Board. At that early period they thought the new chance had come and that they would be helping to bring a better spirit to mining. How do they feel today when anyone working for the Board is classed as almost as much an enemy as the old owners? Without doubt the machine has rolled them into shape for they have made up new homes amongst strangers, and have left the old attachments.

I have watched, from outside, the way a couple of managers who tried to be fair and just have got on. Their path has been difficult. There are a section of the workers who take advantage of any decency and although the majority may respect such a manager, others will badger and twist so that any reasonable attitude to their claims is impossible. After all, a manager is responsible for safety and he may lose his certificate. He must also make the colliery pay so he must overbear those loud talkers who are expert hagglers but uneager workers. Unless you could have a strong committee working in conjunction with the management I cannot see much chance for a democratic management.

If nationalisation is to succeed it must have a dedicated management and workers who understand why they are working and what are the aims – and the results of failure. They should have an inspiration to work even harder than under private ownership. If they treat it as a source from which easy money and soft jobs can be gained then it cannot succeed. I know that the administrative side showed a bad example by trying for the feathered part of the nest at the start, and so the average man could not be so much blamed for getting what he could out of it while all the others were doing likewise. Our union did not seem to realise that the top career men in the industry were guarded by good advisers who warned them that their big money racket might be queried before long and so they were given the safeguard against dropping – they made long contracts. If you do a job wrongly the first time and have to re-do it, that makes things harder for the first errors must be cleared and properly rebuilt. So it will be with any attempt to reorganise mining nationalisation.

Anyway, I think it is a fading industry. In the not too distant future the dirt and toil of coal mining and using will be abandoned and a safer, cleaner world will result. Some coal may be needed for the by-products but the tonnage will be small in comparison.

SHORT STORIES

INTRODUCTION

It was the publication of his short story 'The Flame' in 1937 that first made Coombes known to a wider audience and earned him acclaim as an important new writing talent. His powerful, graphic, stark, and at times even uncompromising stories which were published in the late 1930s were widely praised: John Lehmann was particularly impressed by 'the simplicity and unforced, quiet movement of the writing . . . allied, as story after story showed, with a capacity to make you feel exactly what it was like to be alone in a mine'. Although Coombes was hailed as a short-story writer of great ability and potential, and was often encouraged to write more in this genre, it was a promise he never fulfilled. After the late 1930s and early 1940s he does not seem to have composed many more stories. Indeed, some of those which appeared in *Coal* magazine in the late 1940s were revised versions of earlier compositions.

Among Coombes's papers is a bound volume entitled 'Fragments . . . Short Stories', dated 1935–6. This contains a number of short stories, and short plays for theatre and radio, which were written by Coombes when, under the pseudonym 'Becomb', he was a member of the 'British Scribbler' writing circle. Some of the stories were circulated among other members for comment, and the resulting responses, which are generally favourable in nature, are also included in the volume. Valuable testimony regarding the contemporary impact of Coombes's early writing, as well as of the literary forms, subject matter and styles he initially experimented with, have thus survived.

The stories in the 'Scribbler' volume vary in quality. Passages in some of them reflect Coombes's efforts to master syntax, grammar and clarity of expression, whilst others labour with unpromising ideas. It is hardly surprising perhaps that the life and character of mining communities feature prominently yet Coombes was not averse to experimenting with different contexts: one story, 'Always', is a not altogether successful treatment of a single landscape in three historical episodes: Stone Age, contemporary and futuristic.

Of the four short stories we have selected for inclusion in this anthology three are taken from his 'British Scribbler' volume: 'The Inheritance', 'Fate' and 'The Watch'. The date on the volume strongly suggests that these were written *c.*1935–6, though they may well have been completed earlier. As well as being among the best of the previously unpublished stories in the 'Scribbler' volume, these three have interest from the point of view of their subject-matter. In 'The Inheritance' Coombes drew on some of the harsher features of rural life, of which he had direct experience, whilst 'Fate' examines an episode from the viewpoint of a woman in the mining valleys, an uncommon perspective in the literature of the time. Both 'Fate' and 'The Watch' were also the stories most favourably commented upon by the Club's respondents and tutors. Some of its contemporary readers regarded 'The Watch' as 'excellent and well-constructed' and 'gripping' and as proof that as a writer Coombes 'should certainly look forward with confidence'.

The other story presented here, 'His Message', has survived in loose form, partly revised, and typed on the obverse side of drafts of other works. Its composition is harder to date though it is highly likely that it was also written during the same period. It is included here partly because in some respects it anticipates the subject-matter, style and technique of the published stories 'The Flame' (which also centres on a character named Jack Davies) and 'Machine Man'. All three feature miners being killed or narrowly escaping death in unexpected circumstances while they work alone underground. Of particular interest is the graphic and vivid step-by-step description of Jack Davies lifting the block of coal into the tram. This device succeeds in involving the reader intimately in the action and is again exploited to the full in 'The Flame' and 'Machine Man' as imminent death approaches the protagonists of those two stories.

His Message

~

JACK DAVIES knew it was along the tunnelled roadway that any help must come, but he saw no sign of a light when he peered into the darkness. Everything was as black as it can be half a mile below the surface of a mountain.

Jack's lamp, hanging on a post, gave the only light that brightened the surroundings. On his right side the iron of the coal tram showed grey in the feeble light; the smudge of chalk markings showed as a muddle of figures cancelled by the last one.

In front of Jack, stretching into the darkness on both sides, was the nine feet of height in which the Big Vein shone and glistened when his light showed the slips in the coal of that anthracite seam.

The cloud of dust settled slowly, very slowly, for Jack had that minute paused from throwing the coal into the tram. It was full, level with its sides, now Jack wanted to place lumps around the edges so that more coal could be thrown into the centre. One lump was lying near his feet; it was a large piece of coal, square and solid. Its weight could not have been much less than three hundredweights.

'There's no sign of a blinkin' soul,' Jack complained to a space between the tram and the lump. 'There never is when a bloke wants a bit of help, no fear. Looks as if I'll have to struggle and get it up meself, eh?'

He had the habit of speaking his thoughts aloud for he mostly worked by himself and he found comfort in an imagined companion to whom he could tell his complaints. If his mates heard Jack talking to himself they told one another that 'Jack have got old Charlie down with him agen.' Charlie existed only in the shadows of the mine.

'By good rights I did oughter break it smaller, see?' Jack informed the darkness, 'but it 'ud take a lot of pounding to crack it

and then most like it 'ud go all to small. They won't pay nothing
for small so I gotter get it up like this somehow.'

He tumbled the lump over until it was near the side of the tram;
it took all his strength to roll it.

'Aye indeed,' he assured the darkness, 'it'll take some lifting – it
will that.'

He hitched up his trousers, then set his feet for the lift. He had
only a singlet with no sleeves on the upper part of the body and his
skin shone like ebony with its coating of small coal mixed to a
paste with his sweat.

Jack bent swiftly and his biceps muscles swelled out when he
placed his arms around the lump and began to lift. He gasped and
grunted when it started to come up in his arms; the rough edges of
the lump grazed his skin. Three inches – then six inches – he lifted
it and every inch was a strain. When it was up twelve inches he
could ease the weight on the rim of the tram wheel so that he
could get ready for another lift. Another effort he made, then it
was high enough for him to take some of the weight on his bended
knee. In another few seconds he had it waist high, then he could
use his strength more directly. He pressed his body against the
coal and with an upward push he worked it along until it was chest
high and almost level with the top edge of the tram.

Then the last three inches, by far the hardest of them all. At that
height he could not get a leverage for his arms, and he had used his
first strength. His arms were aching and tiring, too. He began to feel
doubtful whether he could get the lump up that little way further, or
whether it would crash back down on him, perhaps on to his feet. It
was on the balance for some seconds while Jack was straining to find
the strength to push it over the top. He held it between the tram and
his chest while he rested, then when the lump seemed about to slip
down again he made a final effort. His breath hissed through his
clenched teeth as he forced the lump up fraction by fraction until it
was balancing on the tram edge. There it wavered back and fore
until Jack was able to let the weight of his body fall against the lump
to force it over on to a resting place among the smaller coal.

'By Gosh!' Jack gasped, then leaned against the tram while he
drew the back of his hand across his eyes to divert the sweat that
was running into them; 'That was most too much for me, that one
was. No sense in lifting a lump like that. Could see sparks in front
of my eyes, so I could.'

Then he felt cold and his skin was wet and clammy. The drops of sweat felt like touches of ice when they fell on his chest. His breathing became laboured; his chest went up and down in straining movements that shook his shoulders. Suddenly the tram seemed to move away from him – his knees trembled then sagged under him. The single electric light went dim, then shot into a glaring red, then became a dancing movement of streaking light.

'Gawd!' Jack's comment was soundless then; 'What's a happening to me? Feels mighty queer, so I do.'

Then he realised that the lamp was still in the same position; he was swaying himself; the tram was solid and still. The heaving in his chest was getting worse; his eyes felt to be bursting; the pain from them travelled through his neck to his chest and heart.

'I've done it. Aye, I've done it.' Jack was sure then, as the place started to move about him afresh. 'Strained me heart, that's what I've done – and I'm finished I knows I am.'

He lost the power in his legs and was forced to hold to the side of the tram. But his brain kept clear. He thought that death must be near to him and knew that no help could arrive in time. He could feel the burning course of each pulse as the heart forced its load of blood. He was a strong and determined man. He had something to do before he died and meant to do it.

His thoughts were for his wife and children. He knew that if he was found there, as he was, the verdict would be that his death was caused by heart failure; he had known cases when it had happened that way. That would mean that his wife and family would get no compensation. That should not happen, on that he was determined; he would put them as right as he could. If he died alone he meant to leave a message for others to read.

With his left hand clenched over the tram, he put his right into his pocket and pulled out a lump of chalk. He swayed between every action but defied collapse until he was done. He hurried because he felt he had so little time but the white message showed very clearly against the dirty sides of the tram.

'Lifted too big a lump. Strained heart. J.D.'

When he finished the last letter his strength gave and he slid down. The tram, with its message, stood above his head like a tombstone. Even when he was on the floor he fought the dizziness so that he should be doubly sure. Near his tram there lay a wide curling box made of strong tin; Jack stretched across to it then started to chalk again.

'Too big a lump. Strained . . .', the chalk rolled from his hand as Jack shuddered, then lay still.

The lamp light shone on the grey whiteness of his face as he lay there with his head and body bedded in the small coal. Gas worked behind a slip of coal; it rumbled like slow thunder as it forced its way along; then the coal was burst out with a crash and it fell, showering the ground with the smaller lumps and filling the air, which was scarcely moving, with choking dust. Almost above the head of the motionless man a post split and then broke clean in half. It made a noise like a pistol shot but Jack did not move. It seemed that the only silent thing in that tomb was the man. The coal, the roof, and the timber were creaking and moving under the pressure of the ground above.

Out of the darkness behind the man's head two eyes shone, then a small grey shape slid forward into the light. It halted a yard away from the prostrate man. Another grey shape moved forward, then another, and another, until the small coal appeared to be alive with rustling movements. Then the first rat bit at something near the man's ear and another leapt to take it from him. There was a sharp squeal.

The Inheritance

~

'The meek shall inherit the earth' –

PERHAPS.

Over forty years ago old Tom Gelder had come to the little cottage in Stoney Lane. He was 'young Tom' then, newly married – and very proud of his home and Sarah his wife. At six o'clock the next morning he had started across the fields to work at Green Meadow Farm, with a hunk of bread and cheese in his pocket, and at dark he returned. Over forty years passed, and still he travelled the same road. Surely no man had ever been meeker than he; yet it seemed all the earth he would ever inherit was the amount he brought home with him on his corduroy trousers.

He was a cattleman, and a good one too. He loved the animals under his care, and tended them well when they were ailing. Now, after all those years, he had learned more of anthrax and milk fever than anyone for miles around. If there was trouble at calving time, they always sent for old Tom Gelder. He would amble over with a smile on his round face, and gratefully accept the drink of cider given by the relieved farmer. It saved paying the veterinary surgeon a guinea!

True, things weren't so easy when the two boys were growing up. It was a job to get them clothes, and often Tom used to carry the same piece of cheese about for days – just looked at it, then ate the bread and put the cheese back for the next day. But it was worth it. They grew into fine boys. His heart was glad the day he saw the two of them in khaki, and the Squire stopped on the road to tell him how proud he was of them.

Somehow, after they'd gone, there didn't seem anything to hurry home for. Sarah kept getting more fidgety and quarrelsome,

71

and took less interest in her home and husband than ever. He got into the way of not coming home until it was so late that there was only time to drink a cup of tea, have some sort of supper, and go to bed.

And yet, after all, those intervening years had not been so dreary. Into his life had come an unexpected ray of hope, which his loneliness fanned into a flame that dominated his life and thoughts.

He had heard of it happening to others, so why shouldn't it happen to him? Gradually, because he had nothing else to look forward to, he had decided that there was no doubt it would come true. Sometimes he would chuckle aloud at the thought, and the men working near him would give a startled glance in his direction. But they'd look more startled still when it became a fact, thought old Tom. For it was no small thing that kept his heart cheerful and his eyes always bright.

It was a long time since she had told him. One night, when that feckless Kitty Williams had dropped in for the usual gossip, she had said:

'Let me read your fortune in the cup, Mr Gelder.'

'Don't hold wi' it,' Tom had objected.

'Oh, come on! There's no harm, and look at all the tea-leaves left!'

She had taken the cup from his unwilling hand and shaken it. After studying the inside, she had sat back with an astonished squeak.

'Laws, Mr Gelder! If this bean't the luckiest cup I ever seed! I can see wannerful things for you in 'ere!'

'Huh!' growled Tom sceptically.

'Aye, it's right enough, and as plain as a pikestaff. See this!' and the pointing finger indicated a cluster of leaves. 'A fine carriage coming for you, with gentlemen in it. There's their heads. And a long journey – and see, a big 'ouse at the end of the journey! It's all 'ere. Can't you see it?'

He couldn't see it, and didn't believe it. Yet when Kitty had gone and he sat thinking it over, he was less doubtful. Stranger things had happened. Perhaps that uncle who had gone to America had become rich and would leave his money to him. Or – and his eyes grew misty – perhaps he would have some news of his boys after all these years – perhaps they would come and take him away with them.

And all the passing years had failed to kill that forlorn hope. But he wished it would come true soon, for he was getting feeble, and was slower than ever at his work. So slow that his master – he was the old master's grandson – had told him that he would have to get a younger man. And his head had ached cruel of late, and it was a job for him to hobble to his work. Never mind; his master would be welcome to get another man when that fortune came!

Tom's chuckles became more frequent, and he avoided his fellow-men and kept more to his cattle.

~

Then came that morning when he never woke until gone eight o'clock. That was queer, because as long as he could remember he had got up at five and made his own breakfast.

When he struggled downstairs the cottage was looking remarkably clean and tidy, and his breakfast was ready. The feeling of strange alarm still stayed with him. Then he stared open-mouthed at his boots, for some attempt had been made to brush them and scrape off the thick caked mud.

He had not recovered from this last surprise when Sarah entered, followed by Kitty Williams.

'Oh, you've got up, have you?' said his wife.

'Aye. Why didn't you wake me?'

'Well, I knew you was mortal bad last night.'

'But them cattle? They've got to be fed.'

'Now rest yourself. We sent a message to say you was ailing, and they're going to manage.'

But it was no use. The regular habits of a lifetime are not so easily broken, and he felt miserable. And that queer feeling that something was going to happen was upon him all the time. The house so clean, and his boots; and Sarah much quieter than usual and not so snappy. He thought she looked as if she had been crying. And Sarah hadn't looked like that since – since those two long letters had come from the King. Something about 'Missing, believed killed'.

~

'Where are you going to now?' she asked.

'Out for a walk,' answered Tom, with his hand on the gate.

'Well, if you do, you want to be here when they come.'

'When who come?' he queried suspiciously.

His wife hesitated, and Kitty slipped in with a glib explanation.

'We wanted to surprise you. Two gentlemen came to inquire about you yesterday, and they said they'd come back today. They wanted to see you particular, and they might be here any minute now.'

'Was they in a car?'

'Yes, a fine big car, and they said they wanted you to go with 'em to-day if you could,' and Kitty squeezed his arm in new-found friendliness.

He was not greatly surprised. He had been waiting years for it, and it was working out exactly as he had thought it would. Now he must be careful how he behaved. Mustn't let them think he didn't know what to do. So, shortly after, when a big car backed up to the garden gate, he was apparently more interested in the currant bushes near him at the top of the garden.

Yet he was quite aware that the two women were talking to the occupants. One of the two men in the back of the car got out. After a pointed glance in Tom's direction, this man came down the path towards him.

'Mr Gelder?' he inquired very politely.

'Aye,' replied Tom, after he had got over his surprise at being called Mr Gelder by such a well-dressed gentleman.

'Mr Thomas Gelder?' pursued the gentleman, who seemed a little at a loss.

'Yes, that's me. Do you want me to come with you now?'

'Yes, if you would. Oh, don't bother about changing your clothes,' for Tom had been eyeing his corduroy trousers and comparing them with those of his visitor. 'We'll soon fix you up for that. No trouble at all. Your wife can come on later – we're in a bit of a hurry, you see. Oh, no, not in there. Come sit in the back seat with us.'

And Tom settled back to enjoy his first ride in a car and the cigarette they had given him. It was great, flying along the road like that! And to think that he'd be able to do it every day, and have no more masters to bully him!

There was a fine big house behind the trees. They turned in. A man in uniform opened the gated and saluted as they passed.

'Any trouble?' asked the uniformed lodge-keeper as he re-opened the gates for the empty car a few minutes later.

'No, none at all. Poor old josser, he came like a lamb. Seemed to think a dream had come true or something. Quite harmless, the doctor said; only he'd had too much watery cider and not enough good food. Well, I must be off.'

And the gates of the mental hospital closed with a loud clang.

Fate

~

IT seemed that something checked the call on the woman's lips. She turned from the bottom of the stairs to walk back into the kitchen, her mouth still partly open, one hand pushing the greying hair from her forehead. The other hand groped for a chair; finding one, she dropped into the seat with a sob of relief. For possibly two minutes she sat, elbows in front of her tightly-closed mouth, then got to her feet.

She stayed still as she glanced across the table, breakfast already laid on it, and her eyes passed to the pit clothes, ready near the fire. She noticed the time on the clock and started to mutter to herself, as some do who are much alone.

'Nearly six; I must call Jimmy. Yes – everything's ready – I must call – But something seems to stop me; I – I feel so giddy – I'll – '

She walked unsteadily to the door and opened it, drawing in the fresh air. She stood and watched the morning light grow stronger; a few lights still showed in the mining village below; the faint sound of the engines at the pit bank reached her ears.

Ah! that was better – the cool air had revived her – now she must call Jimmy. She turned away from the door, and as she did so the colliery siren shrieked out a staccato warning to the lie-a-beds.

It was merely the usual warning that the last minute for getting up had come, but in her upset condition that sudden shrill blast had shaken the woman's every nerve. Ghastly white and trembling, she closed the door to shut out the sound and then sank into the nearest chair – a realisation of the meaning of her mood had come to her. Fifteen years before on such a morning and at the same hour she had gone through the routine. Then it had been for Jim, her husband, Jimmy's father. She had had that queer, frightened feeling that morning too – had told Jim of it – but he had tried to laugh her fears away.

'Why, lass, if we took notice of fears, we wouldn't work one day a week. Then what about young Jimmy and you? – and what about the pantry?'

He had gone off with a laugh that early morning, but he had not come back to her alive; the pit had had its way.

But this second warning should not be ignored; she owed it to her dead husband – perhaps the warning had come from him.

The sound of the engines seemed to grow in intensity, until they seemed to her like the roar of demons clamouring for more men to deliver to their fellows in the depths, where they would be crushed to pieces.

But she would not pay a second toll. She would cheat those monsters of their prey. Sound asleep, Jimmy would not wake until she called him; and she would not call him until it was too late. She put the working clothes back in the cupboard, getting some pleasure from the act, and sat down to wait.

But alone with her thoughts she felt terrified. Jimmy was all she had in the world, and in her fear she wanted to be near him – to guard him. Silently she went up the stairs, listened outside his room, then, when she caught the sound of his regular breathing, entered and sat at his bedside. She watched his features lovingly, seeing in them the memories of that young husband whom death had snatched from her.

Sitting there, so near him, she calmed a little. By the time it was too late for him to go to work she was almost herself again, and went back downstairs. Soon after, she called him. Sensing it was late, he came down very quickly and his eyes noted the time.

'But mother,' he asked, reproachfully, 'why didn't you call me? You know we can't afford to lose time.'

'I know, son – I know that well. But somehow I was upset this morning and left it too late – come and have your breakfast, it's waiting.' Jimmy tackled his breakfast, as usual, in good spirit.

'Can't make out what came over you this morning, mother,' he said when he had almost finished.

'I don't know – perhaps it was the fine morning – the smell of spring. It made me long to be back in the country.'

'Still thinking of it, mother?'

'Oh! Jimmy. How I have longed to go back to Resford. We – we were born there, your father and I, and we always talked of going back as soon as we could save a little money. His parents lived in the village, mine a little farm just outside.'

'Gosh', said Jimmy, 'but I'd like to see that village.'

'It was very nice there. Towards the village, from our house, was a long, wide, bank; and in the spring it was covered with primroses. At the end of the bank was a knoll, with four big trees, one at each corner; we used to call it the Bower – there was a crossroads there, I remember – we used to meet there – bluebells were covering it when – I'm sure it would be covered with them now, and I haven't seen one for years.'

'No, mother; they don't grow anything much except small coal and ashes here.'

'Have you finished breakfast?'

'Yes, thanks, mother; – After all it's a treat to be out of the mine on such a fine day as this. It isn't often I get a day in the sunshine. How far away is Resford – that village you were talking about?'

'Let's see – about eighteen miles I think; but it might as well be eighty.'

Jimmy went out. Presently, as she moved about doing her house-work, his mother could hear the sound of tinkering in the shed.

Some time later she went out to the shed and looked in; he had gone, and taken the bicycle with him. His mother smiled; the ride – she had intended putting the idea into his mind – would do him a deal of good.

The morning went on; Mrs Davies busied herself with her work. Suddenly she noticed the time.

'My goodness – quarter to one – and haven't made dinner; Jimmy will be here with a big appetite now,' and she hurried to the back door with the kettle.

So startling that it caused her to jump and spill the water, the hooter blared out again.

'Our clock must be slow, that's one o'clock,' she tried to persuade herself; 'but no – it's keeping on.' It was – no sharp staccato blast this time but a sustained shriek that continued until it seemed that it would never end. She knew its message, as did all the others. There was disaster in the pit; that hooter was to summon rescue parties and other helpers to the scene as quickly as possible.

Her cottage was higher than the village. Already she could see half dressed men, women with white, frightened faces, and wondering children hurrying to the top of the pit. In a flash she realised that her instinct had once again been right; but for it, one more would be down. She left her cottage and hurried into the village. Mrs Hughes, her neighbour, was there too.

'Isn't it terrible, Mrs Davies; more than forty still down, they can't get at them, blocked in, they are.'

A workman, eyes gleaming sombrely from a black face, told them snatches of news. Yes, it was in the South district, where Jimmy worked – no there was no fire as yet – if they could get to them before the air went – but they wouldn't know anything definite for an hour or so, p'raps two hours –

'I think I'll go home, Mrs Hughes;' she said a little later, 'perhaps Jimmy has come home, and I can't do anything here. If they have any news before I come back, call and let me know. I've got a lot of clean blankets and towels ready – if they're needed send to fetch them.'

Back in her house she found Jimmy had not returned. She ate a little dinner herself, and put her son's ready in the oven. Then she took the blankets and towels from the chest in preparation for taking them along. As she did so she noticed a big car stop outside her door.

'Mr Rees, the colliery owner,' she muttered, surprised, 'I expect he hasn't heard that Jimmy isn't in work – or he wants me to go and help in the houses.'

She put the blankets on a chair, gave a few touches to her hair and clothes, and opened the door as the knock came.

'Oh! Mr Rees; please come in.'

'Thank you, Mrs Davies.' He took off his hat and came in slowly.

'I've been preparing some sheets and things, I thought –'

'Then you've heard, Mrs Davies – I hardly knew how to tell you.'

'About the explosion, Mr Rees? Yes I heard and I'm going down there now.'

'No, about – about your boy – Jimmy.'

'Oh, Jimmy isn't in work today. I persuaded him to go for a ride in the country.'

'Yes,' Mr Rees hesitated, 'he – he went to Resford, and they telephoned me to come quickly because of the explosion here. As we passed the crossroads near the Bower your boy came out on his cycle – we couldn't help hitting him – he died in my arms and his last thoughts were for you – he made me promise to give you these.'

He handed a big bunch of bluebells to the mother.

'Mrs Davies – Mrs Davies.' Mrs Hughes was shouting from the yard gate, and her call was glad and loud enough to pierce even the numbness that had overcome Mrs Davies. 'Oh, there you are at last. There's no need for you to go down again; they've had them all up safe.'

The Watch

~

'FOXY' Bates came to the corner, checked himself, and stood irresolute. The lights that appeared just in front warned him that he was nearing a small town, while the fading moonlight convinced him that he would not see to make his way alongside the mountain wall much longer. He would soon be compelled to descend and travel the road that led into that cluster of lights, or stay on the mountain side until the early dawn would enable him to make his way furtively to that not very distant city where he knew of safe refuge.

He stood on a raised incline, the darkness of which cut through the mountain grass like a wide shadow, running straight down towards the road half a mile below; the sheltering stone wall went forward at right angles to it. Whatever happened, he must avoid that road, for very likely they were watching for him there. Yet the alternative of staying some hours on the boggy mountain side was not a pleasing one to a man whose exhausted body craved sleep. He turned and looked upwards to where the contrasting incline cut its way towards the crest of the mountain.

As he looked, the moon sailed into a last stretch of clear sky before disappearing into the dark clouds, and in that brief brightness he saw, far up the mountain, a group of buildings that clearly formed the end of the incline. Even the winding gear of the colliery there was visible. Much nearer him, not more than a hundred yards away, was a single large building standing alongside the incline. It had not the shape nor the whitewashed exterior of the mountain farmhouses. The moonlight went out as quickly as snuffed candlelight, but no gleam from that building pierced the darkness.

The man walked carefully up the incline, between the two pairs of narrow-gauge rails that were laid on it, and cautiously neared the building. Around and inside it all was silent. He saw a door at the farthest end, but did not go on to it because a door might creak, and the need for caution was urgent. Nearer him was a window, as big as the side of an ordinary room. It was without glass, but the steel frames were intact. With practised skill he lifted himself up and slid quietly inside. His guess that it had been an engine house was right, for in the part where he found himself, the raised concrete bedding of the engines was still there with the iron standards embedded in it. At the inner side he found a recess between the wall and the concrete. Knowing it would be warmer there, and out of sight from the window, he placed the bundle he carried as a pillow, pulled some rotten sacking he found there over him as he lay down, and was soon fast asleep.

~

A split second before, he had been sleeping; even now his eyelids were only open the merest slit – but he was awake, with every sense searching the darkness for the reason for his awakening, while his breath still came steadily, changing every now and then to the louder puff of a sleeping man. 'Foxy' was acting up to his name. Of late it had not been the method of his sleeping that had mattered to him, only the manner of his waking. Now, with no perceptible movement, his head was slowly turning on the bundle, and from under those lowered eyelids, keen startled eyes were scrutinising every object as it came within his vision.

Over the engine bed he could see the skeleton window, and noted that the bright moonlight of the earlier night had gone; a grey mistiness showed instead. The time, he guessed, was somewhere between two and three o'clock. Whatever had disturbed him? There did not seem to be anyone near. Satisfied on that point, he put out his hand to raise himself, and with difficulty checked a cry as he touched something wet and sticky.

He was on his feet without a sound, drawing the shaking hand towards his eyes in an effort to see what was on it; but it was his sense of smell that reassured him.

'Oil!' he muttered. 'Oil, was it? I thought it was blood.'

Yes, since that call at the lonely farmhouse two days ago he had been seeing blood. The scene flashed before his eyes as it had done scores of times. The feeble old woman talking as she went inside.

He knew that old trick, pretending there was someone there. He had taken one step into the passage and looked around the door. She was searching in a small tin box in the dresser drawer; he watched her take sixpence out before pushing the box to the back of the drawer and covering it with a cloth. As she closed the drawer, he stepped outside. He noticed how she trembled when she brought him the sixpence and a piece of bread and cheese – how she was trying to please him.

'If you'll wait here a minute I'll bring you a cup of tea. I'm making one for my sons. They're out at the back.'

More bluff: if she had any sons it was plain they were nowhere close. What did an old woman like her want to hoard money for? When the rattle of cups showed she was busy in the back kitchen, he had stepped into the other room, slid the drawer out, and grabbed the box. He lifted his head at a sound from the door; the old woman was there. The cup of tea crashed from her hand as she came forward with surprising speed for one so old. He flung her sideways as she tried to snatch the box back, but she came again, her bony hands clawing at his eyes, grey hair down over her face, a terrible screech issuing from her dry wrinkled lips. He drove the box full into her mouth, and as she fell, hitting her head against the open drawer, he scooped out the four pound notes and some silver, pushed the empty tin into the drawer, and closed it.

He stepped over her as she lay there, a pool of blood by her mouth. That blood, that last gasping cry as she fell, had haunted him ever since; it had ended in a sort of smothered sob like . . .

His muscles tautened, the lifted bundle dropped from his fingers; in the darkness his mouth fell open and his eyes distended, for he had heard that sound again. He made one panicky step towards the window, hitting his leg against an iron standard, then checked himself. It might have come from outside, and then he would jump right into danger. Perhaps those two men who shouted to him as he left the farmhouse had followed him, for the old woman had not lied about her sons. He must not rush blindly out, but get away he must.

'Foxy' lifted his bundle again, then moved inch by inch towards the doorway in the corner; he squeezed past the half of a door that was left; his groping fingers touched and followed a wall and his feet slid silently behind the guiding fingers. He went forward several feet like this, then suddenly checked himself, for a flame had flickered somewhere in front of him, and shone through a wide crack in a door which was not six inches from his face.

As he hesitated the sound came again, the dry choking sob of a tortured being. The listener felt the flesh on his body quiver; his teeth were chattering; but some terrible power compelled him to take that last short step and place his eye to the opening. He watched for a few seconds, then his held-up breath came in a long sigh of relief. Whatever dread thing he had expected, the sight that met his eye was not it.

He saw a room that had once been used as an office or store-room, for a broken desk was on one side, while on the other he saw a door which seemed to be the one he had noticed from outside. Near it stood several old oil drums and a pile of cotton waste. Some of this oil-soaked waste had been piled on the grate, with part of the broken desk put on top, and a smoky blaze was smouldering. An occasional drop of oil would flare up to show a figure that sat near the fireplace, gazing at some small object held in its hand. At intervals a sob would echo through the building.

'A blasted kid,' muttered Bates disgustedly, 'and 'owling!'

He half turned to feel his way back along the passage. At that instant the fire blazed up strongly and the thing in the boy's hand glittered. A startled look came into the watcher's eyes; he pushed the creaking door wide open and entered. The boy rose to his feet with an exclamation of surprise, but as he rose he closed his hand and hid what it held in his pocket. The man smiled to himself as he heard the closing click.

'I – I didn't know there was anyone else here.' The boy's voice showed no fear, only relief at the prospect of company. 'Foxy's' eyes studied the pale wistful features.

'What are you doin' 'ere?' he questioned. 'Why ain't you at 'ome?'

'I haven't got a home,' replied the boy. 'I've been walking all day to get here. You see, we used to live close to here when father was working here. I played in here when I was a boy –' his age could not have been more than fifteen, 'and wait for him to walk home with him.'

'Where's 'e now?' queried the man.

'He – he died when I was just nine years old and mother took me away. She couldn't bear to stay here any longer, and she – she died eight days ago.'

'So you're coming back to yer folks, eh?'

'No. I haven't got any relations either. I came here because I'd been so happy around here once.'

'What's that you've got with you?' persisted Bates.

'Oh, some tea and sugar. I've got a tin. When the fire lights I was going to make a cup of tea. And there's part of a loaf of bread I brought with me yesterday. Would you like a share? Although,' he added, 'I'm afraid it's gone dry.'

'No,' replied 'Foxy', 'I mean that there thing you was 'owling over.'

The boy hesitated, his hand clutching the precious thing in his pocket.

'Come on. Let's 'ave a look at it,' urged the man.

'Oh! Yes.'

He brought it slowly out and held it in the opened palm of his hand. It was a small watch, hardly bigger than half-a-crown, but of gold and exquisitely worked. A wonderful little watch. The man stared, the shadows hiding the greed in his eyes.

'Gawd!' he gasped, then asked, 'Where did you get that from?'

'It was my mother's,' said the boy sadly. He pressed a tiny spring and the back clicked open. 'See, there's her picture on the back. She said dad gave it her for a wedding present.'

'Foxy' looked at it during a brief silence. The one who had given it had not stinted money on his present. It would fetch a long way towards twenty pounds. He made a move towards it.

'I can't see it very well from 'ere,' he complained. 'Let's 'ave a good look at it. Are you afraid to give it in my 'and?'

'I promised I'd never part with it,' explained the boy.

'You won't be parting with it. You'll get it back, only I want to feel it and 'ave a good look at it.'

The boy hesitated a second, then slowly held his hand out.

'Be careful you don't drop it,' he warned.

'I'll look after it all right,' replied 'Foxy' with a grin as he took it. 'It'll be safer with me than with you 'cos I know a safe place to keep it.'

He started to untie the string around the bundle. At first the boy watched anxiously, then came forward.

'Have you finished with it? May I have it back, please?' he pleaded.

''Ave I finished with it?' sneered 'Foxy'. 'Not likely I 'aven't. I'll get a couple o' quid outen it afore I finish with it.'

'But it's mine,' begged the boy, 'all I have.'

'Well, you ain't got it now, and I'm a-sticking to it,' replied the man, 'so shut up and don't make any more fuss.'

In sudden desperation the boy jumped forward, pitting his puny strength against the man's. He seized the hand that held the watch and tried to open it. The man pushed him away with the other hand. He swayed away but kept his hold, and 'Foxy' hit him back-handed across the nose until the blood ran – but still he held on. Then the man pushed his fingers against the boy's eyeballs and pressed; with a moan the lad let go, and staggered back whimpering into the corner.

But as 'Foxy' went on opening the bundle the boy's eyes never left that watch, and as it was being placed in the middle with the notes and silver, he sprang like an animal and grabbed it, clenching it tight in his fist.

'You young whelp, I'll learn you!' snarled 'Foxy'.

He dropped the bundle, cornered and seized the boy, but failed to open the tightly gripped fingers.

'All right,' he grunted, 'there's more ways than one.'

His hands caught around the thin throat.

'Now then,' he snarled, 'give it back, or I'll choke it out of you!'

The boy made no answer, his tortured eyes pleading to an inexorable 'Foxy', whose grip tightened until the breath was coming in bursting gulps – but the clenched grip still stayed on the watch. Suddenly the boy went limp in his hands and slipped into a heap on the floor. With the sound of his falling body came another sound from outside the door: a low murmur as if many voices were coming from a distance, broken by a groan, and the noise of many shuffling feet. Startled, 'Foxy' left the unconscious boy, crossed over and peered through the chink by the door-post. The darkness of the incline was full of men, going almost silently downwards and walking slowly, as if the burdened stretchers they carried were very heavy. They were speaking in whispers, and sometimes a moan could be heard.

'Gawd!' muttered 'Foxy'. 'Something's 'appened up there. I must 'op it or some of them may come in 'ere.'

He returned to the task of robbing the boy; bending, he gave a vicious twist to the fingers. Then, with a strange feeling that he was being watched, he turned his head towards the door. He had not heard it open or shut, yet in the middle of the room, his figure just a shade different in colour to the surrounding blackness, stood a powerful man.

He seemed to have left his work in a hurry, for he still wore a close-fitting skull-cap, below which the thick coal dust had turned his face grey. Both strongly-muscled arms were bare past the shoulders; only a thin singlet covered the upper part of his body.

'Foxy' moved away, rising cautiously to his feet.

'Fell down quite suddenly, 'e did,' he explained. 'Taken bad all at once like.'

The newcomer never answered, but moved forward and bent to touch the boy's face. 'Foxy's' nose caught the smell of dried perspiration as the other passed him. The place seemed full of the singed smell of clothes that had been in a hot oven. The boy stirred to the touch, moaned; he was coming back to consciousness. 'Foxy' knew he must get clear away before the boy could tell his tale, for he did not want to grapple with this new enemy.

'Better git a drop o' water for 'im,' observed 'Foxy'. 'I'll fetch it.'

He sidled towards the door, trying to locate the bundle with his feet in the darkness. Then he took his eyes off the other two for a second while he measured the distance he would have to spring when he got his bundle. When his eyes flashed back to the others he gave a startled gasp, for the man stood before him, his grey face looming through the blackness. 'Foxy' saw him flick his arms with the same action that a cricketer employs when testing the swing of a bat; saw the skin of the shoulders rise as the muscles were flexed. Then he noticed that in that moving hand was a collier's mandril, with the sharpened pin-like points glinting; that it was held by the bottom of the handle in order to get the most leverage for the downward stroke; and that when that stroke came it would be directed at his own brain.

'Foxy's' terrified eyes saw the tightly stretched skin over the man's cheek-bones, looked into the deep sockets of his eyes, and saw death there. He flung up his arm to protect his face and shut out what he saw. The action caused him to stagger back and catch his heels in the bundle, which was right behind him.

But that sharp overbalancing shook off the mesmerised numbness that held 'Foxy'. He gave up the idea of reaching and opening that closed door, he abandoned the precious bundle. Life was everything to him now. As his hand touched the floor he shot himself towards that open door that led to the engine-room. Half stumbling, half running, he went along the dark passage, every second expecting to feel the crunch as the mandril hit him.

He was squealing like a trapped rabbit as he forced his way through the window frame and tumbled in a heap outside. The fall tore the knees of his trousers and grazed the skin beneath; he never stayed or felt the pain, but ran blindly, as he had never run before, towards those lights in the valley below. Every breath was a pant, but he raced on, avoiding the hard incline; the mountain bog held at his feet, but he tore himself free and rushed on, hearing behind him the noise of following feet; fleeing from the scrunch of the mandril and that terrible face. Not until he had reached the shelter of the streets and lost all fear of pursuit did he slacken speed to ease his thumping heart.

'The murdering swine!' he muttered, ''e'd 'ave killed me!'

Gradually he regained his calm and decided that, since he was in the town, he might as well make his way through it to reach the other side before daylight came; it was unlikely that there would be anyone about at that early hour. He went some distance along the main street, bending his head to meet a sudden shower that took the place of the drizzle. A whiff of tobacco smoke warned him of some other presence; he moved quickly sideways, stepping into the dark doorway of a shop and into a policeman, whose temper was not improved by having to drop and step on an enjoyable cigarette.

'Here! What's the hurry?' he demanded. 'About pretty early, aren't you?'

'Yes. I'm in a 'urry. Got an urgent message,' explained 'Foxy', starting to move away.

The beam of an electric lamp exposed 'Foxy' from the muddy torn trousers to the dirty unshaven face.

'Yes,' continued 'Foxy', 'p'raps they'll want you to know too. There's been a bad accident at that colliery up there,' he pointed up the mountain.

'Accident?' repeated the policeman, into whose voice had come a change. He gripped the other tightly by the arm, propelling him along the street. 'Better come and talk to the sergeant. I think there's something he wants to talk to you about.'

'But I saw it,' protested 'Foxy', 'crowds of men and stretchers coming down the mountain.'

The reply was a firmer grip on his arm.

'If you're wise you'll give up fairy tales,' warned his captor, 'and stick to the truth. Everyone around here knows there's been a bad accident up there; an explosion that killed nearly all the men working. But it was over five years ago, and no one's worked there since.'

CASTELL VALE

INTRODUCTION

In about 1934 or 1935 Coombes began writing 'Castell Vale', the first of his many attempts at writing a novel. It is likely that he completed three novels: 'Castell Vale', and two versions of 'The Singing Sycamore', one written in the late 1930s and early 1940s, the other in the late 1940s and 1950s. Not one of these was published. Among Coombes's papers are the complete later version of 'The Singing Sycamore', substantial sections of 'Castell Vale', and disconnected fragments and isolated revised chapters of both. Coombes's sustained ambition to be a novelist, which he expressed on a number of occasions, and his persistent attempt at a full-length imaginative work argue strongly for representation in this anthology. We are aware of the obvious limitations of presenting extracts from a novel, especially an incomplete one, and equally conscious of the uneven nature of some of the material it contains. Nevertheless we have included a selection from the surviving chapters of 'Castell Vale' because of its qualities and its significance and interest from the perspective of Coombes's literary and stylistic development.

'Castell Vale' is set in Rescwm, a mining community located in Castell Vale. It traces the fortunes of Glyn Owens and Myfanwy Darrell, and their developing romance. Glyn is a miner and amateur violin-player who is in an unhappy marriage. Myfanwy, sister of Glyn's workmate Jack, is a nurse who returns to Castell Vale following a period at work in London. The novel presents an early exploration of many themes which would permeate Coombes's writing, both fiction and non-fiction: the life of miners and the people of mining communities; the importance of music and Coombes's own particular interest in the violin, and the desire to return to the land and a rural way of life. 'Castell Vale' also emphasizes the importance of the strongly autobiographical dimension to Coombes's work. Castell Vale itself is clearly a fictional representation of the Vale of Neath, and Rescwm of Resolven, where Coombes was living when he wrote the novel.

(Rescwm would also reappear later as 'Restcwm' in 'The Singing Sycamore' and some of Coombes's published short stories, and as 'Treclewyd' in *These Poor Hands*.) Finally, the extracts that follow have interest because they contain the first development of episodes which were later refashioned for inclusion in his later published works. An example of this is the scene in which Jack and Glyn succeed in finding a job, which is also incorporated into *These Poor Hands*.

It is difficult to trace the history of the writing of 'Castell Vale' and its subsequent fate with precision. We do not know if it was ever sent to a publisher, whilst it is possible, though not very likely, that the novel was never completed and Coombes wrote individual chapters out of sequence. About half of the original twenty-one chapters have survived – chapters one and two, four to ten, sixteen, nineteen and twenty-one – although the final pages of some of these extant chapters have been lost. More probably, however, the paper on which the missing chapters were typed was recycled by Coombes for later use. The surviving pages show little traces of revision beyond minor amendments, suggesting perhaps that Coombes abandoned 'Castell Vale' and moved on to other projects. (As we have seen, he completed another novel by the end of the decade.)

It is equally difficult to speculate on the literary merit of the complete work. The survival of an almost full run of early chapters, of isolated subsequent chapters (especially the final one), and a small number of fragmented pages means a very general impression of the overall plot can be roughly pieced together, though obviously key episodes and scenes have been irretrievably lost. The pattern of the first ten chapters, the nature of the narrator's occasional interjections, the seemingly un-necessary diversions, and the general social-reportage style of writing suggest that Coombes was as interested in scene-setting as in unfolding the plot. In its barest outline, at least to the extent that it can be determined, the plot may seem improbable and rather contrived. The surviving extracts of 'Castell Vale' can also imply that, for Coombes, developing the main characters was of less importance than conveying to readers something of the landscape, atmosphere and activities of mining communities in south Wales and the tragedies, hopes, aspirations, fears and humour of their inhabitants. Indeed it could be argued that one of the central themes of 'Castell Vale' is the struggle of Glyn and Myfanwy to overcome conditions that Coombes believed denied working people their true potential, and the two characters' eventual triumph in attaining those cultural values and pursuits that he regarded as being the higher things in life.

What survives of 'Castell Vale' then, betrays many of the flaws that would bedevil Coombes's later efforts at novel-writing. Coombes did not possess all the attributes needed to write full-length fiction of high quality, and this is as apparent in the surviving manuscript of 'The Singing Sycamore' as it is in the extracts reproduced here. He was reluctant to develop his characters and he lacked narrative vision and drive, confirmed perhaps by his own words when he once stated that compared with short-story writing, in a novel 'you can ramble a bit'. It should also be remembered that as well as being Coombes's first attempt at full-length fiction, 'Castell Vale' probably contains some of his earliest writing in any genre, which might explain the rawness and inexpertise which is evident in places. Nevertheless the following selection also contains some memorable passages of acutely observed, and often humorous, writing which brings to life the suffering, dignity and humanity of the people of the mining valleys during the inter-war years.

Partly out of considerations of space and partly in order to sustain coherency, the following section presents in their entirety the first, second, and fourth to eighth chapters of 'Castell Vale'. To avoid confusion they have been renumbered consecutively one to seven. The endings of those chapters whose final pages have been lost have been edited, and, for functional and contextual reasons, we have also provided brief notes regarding the possible contents of the missing third chapter and of the remainder of the novel.

Chapter One

~

ACROSS the wide valley the fog slowly lifted. As it rose, sunshine filled its place, winking from the dew on the grass and shining on the rows of small whitewashed cottages that lined the lower slope of the mountain. Then, rising higher over the church steeple, it passed the tree-dotted park and peeped through the avenue at the hollow where Derwyn House nestled.

An old fox trotting upwards along the Roman Road quickened his pace as the light gained on him, while two seagulls circling around the battle cairns at the top of Craig y Llyn mountain sighted the sea and flew straight down the valley towards it.

Low down, near the river, a thick curtain of mist still hung. It seemed that Nature, having exposed to man's view the beauty of Castell Vale, was now anxious to delay until the last minute the revealing of what was hidden there at the bottom of the valley. But gradually the shape of the mining village became more distinct. First the upper parts of five big buildings, four of them obviously chapels, the other an institute of some kind, came into sight. Then rows of house chimneys, most of them sending out smoke that helped thicken the fog, then roofs of grey houses became plain, slowly emerging, as if unwilling to face the sun.

Suddenly the early morning peace was shattered, as from a distance the six o'clock hooter shrieked out its unwelcome warning, and from the opposite direction a train whistle replied. Then came another sound, the ring of heavy nailed boots on pavement as their owners hurried along the different streets, some buttoning their clothes, others still chewing a hurried breakfast, but every one of them making his way towards that central spot, the railway station, to meet the 'colliers' train'.

The volume of sound increased as the noise of the coming train became more distinct, and the rush of men as well as the train slowed up at the station platform together.

This 'colliers' train' was an engine drawing four old passenger coaches from which all cushions, straps and racks had been removed. The pictures of views had been taken off, too, but the present users had done their best to replace these by chalking sketches of their own. They nearly all carry chalk to use in their work and as they occupy the same compartment each day it is easy to judge the type of passenger by the drawings. It is very clear that the first one is used by a group of mining students for they have sketched a pair of timbers and calculated air velocity by its measurements and anemometer readings.

The next group do not seem to mind what they draw as long as it is something, and their journey is accompanied by far from complimentary sketches of Cabinet Ministers and policemen, while taking pride of place is a large one of the guard, flag in hand and whistle to mouth. In the next compartment, over the partly rubbed-out name of Hyperion,[1] we are given three home teams to win, Birmingham, Oldham and Swansea.

The guard knows most of the passengers; he has travelled with them hundreds of times and he watches they are all there before he starts, walking the length of the train and looking into each compartment to make sure they are all right. With no technical knowledge of mining he wisely refrains from any comment at the first window.

'I see you haven't finished it yet?' he remarks at the second.

'No! We're waiting till we have enough chalk to draw your nose properly,' comes the quick reply. The guard has no riposte ready for this attack on his looks and so gets a bit back on the football enthusiasts.

'Ha! Ha! That came badly unstuck. I told you it would; you should have listened to me,' he reproves them. He stops at the next and looks with interest at a dark, medium-built man with quick, flashing eyes set in a finely drawn face.

'Hallo! Glyn,' he greets him. 'What's it to be today, fiddles or fractures?' Then he misses someone. 'Why where's Jack this

[1] A thoroughbred racehorse which won the Derby and the St Leger in 1933.

morning? Fancy me not missing a chap his size. It's queer for him to be behind, too. Is he coming?'

'Sure to be. He won't miss today in any case I expect. Because we've all got to bring out tools today.'

'So they tell me. Pity ain't it, I shall miss you chaps. Perhaps they'll knock this train off. I remember when we had eight carriages now it's – Here he comes. What's he got with him, some outsider?'

This train was the only one by which passengers could leave the valley in the early morning. Over two hours later another one would leave, bearing a number of children and young people who, loaded with books and wearing school dress and an important air, were going to the County School. The intervening time would be spent shunting train loads of coal about. Therefore anyone who had a long journey to make and a connection to catch would have to take this early morning train. But they were not of it, as were the workers, they were 'outsiders'.

So it was one of these 'outsiders', and a girl at that, for whom Jack was carrying the case that morning. It was no doubt a heavy case, but in the hands of Jack Darrell it was no encumbrance. The guard had the door of his van open ready; Jack pushed the case inside, placed the guard's unread morning paper on it for the girl to look at, and motioned her inside.

'*Dewch mewn,*'[2] he said, 'this will surely be the cleanest place for you till you reach the junction.' When she turned to thank him the tears welled up in her eyes. Jack hastily joined his mate who had been watching the girl as she stood on the platform. She was barely sixteen, as supple and slim as a young tree yet with the tears of a first parting from home at the back of her eyes and the doubt of what was to come in her heart. Her mother fussed around the booking clerk, worried the guard and gave detailed instructions to the girl. The guard stood between them and the rest of the passengers for the duration of a farewell kiss, then signalled 'right away' and swung in through his doorway.

Through misty eyes the old woman watched the train leave. Glyn turned when her waving hand had passed out of sight.

'The old lady stood it better than most of them, Jack,' he said. 'I thought you were going to miss it.'

[2] 'Come in' in Welsh.

'Overtook them struggling along with that case,' replied Jack. 'It was too heavy for them. And I never like to see these girls going away. It reminds me of how we felt when Myfanwy went. Going away from home to people who don't look at things the same way as we do and laugh at our way of talking. Even if they get a good place they're bound to be homesick. And if they get a poor place, what can they do? They can't come home when everyone is unemployed here and p'raps they've borrowed money to pay the fare. I'm not surprised that some of them do take things that don't belong to them to get home again.'

'Neither am I, Jack, I'm not a bit surprised.'

'That girl's going to service in London. Her father's old Sam Morris. You know him.'

'Yes. He's been idle a long time.'

'I told her the name of the hospital that Myfanwy's at. She'll go there if she wants help. Myfanwy will put her right.'

'Yes, she'll put her right,' replied Glyn confidently.

'We heard from her yesterday. Wanted to know how the fiddler was getting on. Asked to be remembered to you as usual,' continued Jack.

Glyn was very silent for some time. He could see a girl's face. Perhaps not a pretty face, but a face that reflected goodness and kindness even from the smiling grey eyes, and he remembered white strong fingers that could bandage an injury or run a scale on the piano and do both well.

Men go to a hated dangerous job with much the same feelings and actions as the boy who 'crawls unwillingly to school', and the 'colliers' train' seemed to understand and sympathise with the temper of its passengers. It travels forward slowly, giving them every chance to see some of the finest scenery in Wales and making it plain it would like to stop every few yards and have a good look around.

That being against the rules, it crawls on until it leaves its human load at the next small station and starts a puffing climb up the gradient; eventually it disappears into the tunnel that goes through the left-hand slope of Craig y Llyn. By now most of the passengers, Jack and Glyn among them, have left the station and are climbing slowly up the mountain to where the Main Drift is situated.

For some hours to come their talk and actions would not be concerned with trains but with trams. Not the sort that jolt you along the streets of the town, but the four-wheeled, iron-bodied trams that cause a collier when he has a poor place to talk of them in his sleep. If he has a good place though he is inclined to talk about them very loudly, in a public house. These trams are the sort that make weary boys peep over their sides and wonder how many more hundreds of heavy shovelfuls they have to throw in to fill that empty space; that cause sweating hauliers, when the trams have gone 'off the road' several times and they have lifted until there are holes in their backs, to use up all their handy swear words and say –

'I think she's a bad un, Phil. Likely the axle's bent or something?'

'Aye,' replies Phil despondently, 'or the colliery's bent p'raps.'

'Mebbe so,' replies the haulier. 'Anyhow, lend us your chalk and I'll mark it off, so's the blacksmith can see it.'

'What the heck's this?' or words to that effect, says the blacksmith outside some time later. 'Some bloke sending all these crosses to me? Must have fallen in love with me. Do they think we've got nothin' to do 'cept mend trams eh? Here, Jim! Take the big sledge and give it a couple of clouts.'

'Where d'you want me to hit it?'

'Anywhere as long as you make a row.'

Jim looks at the sky, gives two haphazard blows with the sledge, then rubs off the chalk crosses. The tram is tumbled back on to the rails and resumes its worrying journeys.

Chapter Two

~

WHAT a difference can be noticed nearly eight hours later when the working shift is over and the men have hurried down to the station! About this time the 'colliers' train' has left that mysterious place past the tunnel known as the Junction, and with a piercing whistle coming before it and a cloud of smoke following, it rushes out of the tunnel, and with wheels spinning at their fastest, dashes down the slope, to be pulled – with difficulty – to a screaming halt at the station.

The train seems to have left terrible things behind in that wild escape, and keeps panting out steam, as if to impress upon the passengers the need to hurry for it wants to take them from those dangers that are found in dark tunnels, and away to safety and home. As a rule there is no delay on their side either, but on this day they are not so eager as usual. They hang about in groups, hardly recognisable as the white-faced men of the morning for now their faces are coal-black, with eyes and teeth shining out in contrast. A cloud of dust follows their every movement; the carriages are full of it, the platform shows their trail. Glyn and Jack were to one of their friends, a porter whose manner of speaking took Glyn's thoughts to the hanging apple orchards and red soil of Hereford.

'You see,' he explained, 'it bean't only you fellows as'll feel it. They'm closin' the signal-box and standin' off two of they shunters.'

The Main Drift has worked its last shift and closed. Every man has an armful of tools with him, and when at last the train pulls out, the railwaymen wave goodbye with genuine sorrow.

'Goodbye, you fellows. Hope to see you again some time, if things will only get better.'

'Yes! If things will get better? So long.'

'You'll come up as usual after tea, Glyn?' asked Jack when they left the station.

'Yes, I'll be up all right, Jack. I expect it will be a relief to get away from our house, for there's sure to be ructions. I'll be told it's my fault the colliery is on stop and so on,' and Glyn Owens watched his mate climb up the slope before he turned and made his way along the street to his home.

Jack Darrell was a bachelor about thirty-three years of age, tall and powerfully built. Clean living and an early life spent on a farm had given him a strength that was unusual. He had returned from war service to find his father dead, and the little farm that had been his home sold. A letter to Glyn Owens, an old war-time friend, had resulted in Glyn getting him work with him at the Main Drift.

At first it had been necessary for him to lodge in Rescwm. He did not stay there long but the memory of that time still tortured him. He was a man who loved the country and the things that belonged to the fresh air; in Rescwm he lived among people crowded together in insanitary houses, with the quarrels of the next-door neighbours and the crying of their children coming through the walls. One shift followed the other into the same beds and quietness was a thing unknown either night or day.

Glyn lived there, too, and Jack watched his friend, who was passionately fond of music, struggle against every obstacle to perfect himself as a violinist. Their friendship had hardened and grown into something deeper. Then Jack had found a little cottage outside the village and some way up the mountain side. It had been abandoned as 'too lonely', but to him it was a haven. With Glyn's enthusiastic help the derelict garden was cleared, windows repaired, and the exterior of the house whitewashed. When all was ready Jack sent for his mother, and she came.

She was in the garden when Glyn arrived there that afternoon. She was tall and thin, with a very erect way of walking, and a faded linen cap kept the straight grey hair in place. Her face was still weather-beaten from many years of Cardigan's sun and wind, but there was no doubt of the welcome she always gave Glyn. Graig Cottage was a very different place now to what it had been, for Mrs Darrell had insisted on bringing a load of rose tree cuttings, currant bushes and flowers with her. Under her care they had been forced to grow – 'Just to have them ready to take back with us when we go.'

The years had rolled on, but the longing for her native Cardiganshire was still strong. She held aloof from the villagers, and Glyn was almost the only visitor. In fact she looked on him almost as a son, and her face brightened when she saw who was coming.

'So you two are starting to enjoy your holidays early,' she said, and the sibilant 'S's of the Cardigan dialect were very plain. 'I was afraid it was one of those farmers coming for Jack with one of their "thank you" jobs. Farmers they call themselves – and if they want a bit of ploughing done, or a horse broken in, aye, or a scythe sharpened even, they can't do it themselves but have to get my son to do it. And he'll do more in an evening after he comes from work than they'll do all day. Yet the old Government will keep on sending boys from here to learn farming. Learn farming, indeed, when half of them are afraid of the dark! They'll never learn farming, it's got to be in the blood.'

He found Jack at the back of the house, sharpening a saw. Soon after, they started for their walk. The late afternoon was still warm and the air clear. Walking slowly, they reached the top of the mountain by easy stages and were now well over two thousand feet up. Below them, as on a model board, the valley and smaller hills were spread.

Jack lay silent for a time, with his gaze fixed on the distance where the mountains of the Carmarthen Fans could be seen.

'Day-dreaming, Jack?' joked Glyn.

'Aye, still dreaming, for it seems now that dreams are as far as I will ever get. In the better times I used to sit here and think of the money we had saved up, every shilling that we could, and compare it with the distance up here. Thinking we've got half enough, that's about equal to that tree-stump halfway up, see it? Twice as much would bring me up to here, then I'd have enough to take the *mam fach*[1] back home and to that little farm where she always longed to be. But now strikes and stoppages have taken all we had, and all I can do is come up here and look at the hills.'

Glyn watched the broad shoulders of his friend hunch in dejection. He was softly whistling a favourite tune to himself, a

---

[1] Roughly translated as 'dear mother'. In this context *fach* is used in an affectionate not diminutive sense.

habit of his – in fact people knew Glyn was coming before he arrived, as the whistle always preceded him. Not all the bad luck or ill-treatment in the world could take the melody out of his whistle or cause the corners of his mouth to droop for long. He was the first to break the silence.

'You know, Jack, I often think you would've made a good raiding chief in the old days when they used to cross these mountains. You're so big and look so savage when you look towards your old home. But after all, things might be worse for you than they are. You've got a good mother and she keeps things nice for you at home. Look at me, with a wife that sneers and nags at me all the time, and if I try to play myself into a happier mood she starts shouting about messing with that squealing thing again. She flies in a temper every time I try to practise, and oh Lord, you should have heard the language when she found out the Drift had closed down! I was all the idlers and wasters she could put her tongue to.'

For a long time the brooding silence was unbroken. All around the ground was hallowed, for it had borne the feet of the Roman armies and taken the bodies of Welshmen who had died to defend it. The Romans, although anxious to leave this wild country with its rebellious people, still stayed long enough to make that road which can still be traced through the grass and past those big stone cairns.

These cairns are a memorial to the later battles, when Welsh prince fought Welsh prince and when the natives fought those bands of raiders who came over the mountains. Now they are forgotten by men, and only the whispering mountain grass tells the wandering breezes the tale of those who lie there.

After a time Jack spoke again.

'Sometimes I bring George Borrow's book[2] with me and read what he says about Devil's Bridge and Hafod Church. It makes me see over the hills to my home. I'll take mother back there some day, whatever it costs me. It kills me to think of her pining all the time.'

---

[2] A reference to *Wild Wales*. Coombes first read this book during the three-month miners' lockout of 1921. In *These Poor Hands* he describes how he was enthralled by it and he also referred to it in other publications.

'I know how you feel, Jack. I was born in the country too. I can remember when – Gosh! What's this?'

Jack turned on his side and stared.

'Why, it's Tom Brost,' he declared, waving to the distant figure and watching with interest as it approached, for it was enough to interest anyone. It was quite likely that Tom was born within the sound of Bow Bells; anyhow, that is what his accent indicated. But he had a heart above towns, and on every possible occasion would roam the mountain with a well-polished but rarely used gun on his shoulder and a motley collection of dogs at his heels. The few rabbits in the locality must have counted him a nuisance for he took every opportunity of frightening them.

'Just point that gun in another direction, Tom,' asked Glyn as he reached them, 'or perhaps you may shoot something for once.'

'For once!' spluttered Tom. 'Blimey! You should have seen me last Saturday; I – '

'Yes, I heard all about it,' interrupted Glyn.

Note:

The next ten pages of the original typescript are missing so it is not known what Tom's exploits the previous Saturday had been, nor what were the contents of the following chapter. The structure and length of the surviving chapters suggest that the one reproduced here was meant to end with an amusing anecdote about Tom Brost. It is difficult to determine what was in the lost third chapter. No new characters seem to have been introduced and there are no indications in the subsequent chapters as to its content. The opening line of the next surviving chapter implies that in part at least the lost chapter described Jack and Glyn's attempts to find work, and how the poor state of their boots prevented them from walking the long distances to other collieries in the locality.

Chapter Three

~

THEN there was that lucky morning when Glyn and Jack came upon a motorist who had had a breakdown and needed help. They did the dirty work while the car owner stood by and gave instructions; finally the motorist had gone his way, leaving them the richer by half a crown – and what proved in the long run to be much more important, he also left behind the damaged tyre that had caused the delay.

That tyre, lying neglected on the roadside, gave Glyn the idea. They took it back to the village, and that afternoon some of the men had a change of occupation. They gave up their usual game of tippet, or shove button, and fell to with enthusiasm. They cut the tyre to pieces with sharp knives and there then followed a great deal of hammering – in some cases of thumbs and fingers, occasioning much bad language. But the problem of their boots was solved, or at any rate eased. Now thick rubber soles and heels protected their footwear, enabling them to walk comfortably and noiselessly.

One result of this was that Glyn and Jack found it possible to go for a long day's tramp in the hope of getting work. So when dawn came over Craig y Llyn next morning Glyn rose and dressed himself. When he was ready to start, a sudden thought came to him and he went to the other bedroom to look at his sleeping five-year-old son. Glyn was not feeling very cheerful. He had been through so many of these mornings – begging, coaxing, for work that was not to be had and returning to a sneering, contemptuous wife. How many weary and disheartened men have turned to the fresh, innocent face of a child for encouragement? As if aware of his presence, the closed eyelids fluttered open, and the voice he loved asked,

'Where you goin', dad?'

'To look for work, Peter boy. Give me a kiss for luck.'

Glyn went on his way, with the memory of those clinging arms and that moist kiss to help him. He called for his mate and together they walked to the upper part of the valley.

When they reached the first colliery they found that, early as they were, others were before them, and the crowd was being added to every few minutes. The fortunate ones at work on the surface of that colliery must have felt very nervous about the attention they attracted. Each man working had a group of watchers surrounding him, and inquiring as to –

'What time does the manager come up?' or 'Did he know if they were starting anybody?'

One of these workmen was busily squirting oil from a pump into the hubs of tram wheels and giving free advice between each squirt –

'You want to watch the way 'es got 'is bowler 'at on, see (squirt) 'cos if 'es got it on the back of 'is 'ead (squirt) 'e's in a good humour, and it'll be all right to ask 'im (squirt) but if 'e's got it pulled down over 'is eyes (squirt) don't ask 'im anythink, for the love of mike (squirt) for then 'e's in a bad humour and 'e'll cuss you up and down, see?'

He pointed out a man who was sitting by the mouth of the colliery. He was alone and kept looking into the dark hole out of which must come his hopes of a job. The oiler told Glyn that this man had not missed waiting there every day for over a year. A short while later the manager came out from the workings. Glyn watched the man jump up and move towards him, a faint hopeful smile on his face. As he neared, the manager looked at him, shook his head, and went on towards the office without a word. The watcher turned away, to go home and return the next day to continue the vigil.

There were more than a hundred men waiting by the office when the manager reached there; he walked straight up to them, and two of the ones in front tried to speak to him.

'Don't bother me,' he snapped, 'there's no hope, I tell you.' He walked into his office without removing his hat; it was down over his eyes.

'That's finished this place – it's no good staying here any longer. Where shall we go now?' asked Jack.

'I've a secret tip that they're likely to start a couple of men at the South Drift. Let's go there,' replied Glyn, and across the valley to the South Drift they went.

When they got there they passed among the men who were already waiting, and listened to the talk.

'No! The Nine Feet seam here isn't much, neither is the Yard. But they say they're going to open the Two Feet seam next week. Yes, they used to earn good money there when it was working before.'

Glyn's keen ears were taking in the gossip. He knew that this colliery had a good name in the valley because the management was more humane than in most, safety regulations were respected and disputes were rare. It was one of the largest and most up-to-date collieries in South Wales.

'Yes indeed, he's a very decent man, this manager,' one man was saying. 'He's rather short, wears glasses. You can be sure of a decent answer from him anyhow – different from some of them.'

The crowd waiting outside the office had become quite large. Rumours were going around as to the whereabouts of the manager. One said he was in his office, another that he was in the workings, while yet another knew for certain that he had gone away somewhere. Some of the men were plainly trying to get rid of the others by sending them off on a wasted journey.

Glyn, ever curious and restless, left Jack to watch their place in the queue while he wandered around, peering at the huge engines in their well cleaned houses. After a while he came to a narrow passage between two fitting shops and following it down found it led to a pathway that had been worn across the open mountain. He turned to retrace his steps; as he did so, a sound of voices came to him.

'Very well. You'll see to that then, George? Get everything ready to start the Two Feet seam by next week. Eh! What was that? Oh! men you say. Yes – I could have started three or four – but how could I go and pick them out of that crowd? Good day,' and a fair man wearing glasses stepped from a doorway into the passage right in front of Glyn. In a flash, Glyn saw his chance.

'Good morning, sir,' he started.

'Good morning,' came the courteous reply as his two twinkling eyes searched Glyn's face.

'I'm looking for work,' said Glyn, 'do you think there's any chance here?'

'Let me see. What are you?'

'A collier.'

One of the manager's eyes was watching Glyn; the other looked towards that desired pathway he could not reach until Glyn moved out of the way.

'Well – as it happens I could start a collier or two.'

'Here's references, sir.'

'No. No. Don't want them. I always go by a man's face. We will soon find out if you are efficient. All right then, you can start on Monday – you'll want a paper from me.'

He pulled out a booklet and wrote rapidly on a yellow form; Glyn told him his name and address and when he had written them down he handed the form to Glyn.

'Take this to the bottom office, they will sign you on.'

'Thank you, sir. What about my mate – he's waiting outside?'

'Oh, your mate; is he used to the coal?'

'Yes, he's a first-class collier.'

'Right. He can start too. What's his name?'

'Now mind,' warned the manager as he handed the second slip to Glyn, 'not a word to that crowd or they'll be chasing me home. Good day,' and he was gone.

'I can't come, mun, or I'll lose my place,' argued Jack in answer to Glyn's call.

'Never mind your place – give it up.'

'Aye. I may as well I s'pose. It's pretty hopeless with all this crowd here, anyhow,' agreed Jack.

'Where are you going that way?' he asked, a few minutes later, 'this is the nearest way home.'

'I know that. But I want to call at the office to sign on.'

'Don't joke, Glyn. I don't like that kind of joke.'

'I'm not joking – see this.' Glyn showed the slip. 'I saw the manager dodging away and he gave me this to get rid of me,' and he told Jack what had occurred.

A very elated Jack followed his mate into the colliery offices, where four clerks took particulars of previous employment and accidents, and examined them verbally and physically to see whether they had ever suffered from nystagmus or beat knees or hands. Then they had to sign their agreement to certain deductions from their pay if and when it came. The last clerk was a very cheerful fellow – he took the name of their doctor and nearest relative in case of accident or death.

Tired but happy they arrived home and were soon being interrogated by their friends as to 'how they did it', and were begged to 'put a word in for us if you see a chance'. In case they should want them they had the offer of all kinds of miners' tools at bargain prices, as the owners feared they would not need them again, and they did need the money.

Chapter Four

~

THE outside of the South Drift on that following Monday morning resembled a small, but very busy town. The streets were rows of fitting, carpenter, and blacksmith shops; followed by weighbridges and offices for different officials. Along one side, one after the other, stood huge engine houses which held machinery that responded to the continual ringing of the signal bells. Thick steel ropes swung from each engine drum and tightened or slackened at the bell's command.

As Glyn and Jack passed one of the engine houses they saw the engine driver, standing like a pigmy alongside the monster he controlled. A red light appeared over the signal bell. Then the bell rang three times – ting-ting-ting. The driver pulled the reverser towards him with one hand and lifted the throttle with the other, keeping his foot lightly on the brake step. Ting – another single staccato ring, then the throttle and brake came down sharply in one section, while the lever was pulled into neutral. The engine driver reached for a brush with his right hand and swept some small coal that the winding rope had dropped on the floor of the engine house into a heap; then he stretched for a shovel and with it lifted the dirt into a bucket. Not for one moment did his attention move away from that space where the light had glowed.

Jack was interested in a smaller building with two big windows and a red cross painted on the door. Several cupboards were recessed in the white enamelled walls; on one side lay a bath, with shining taps ready to flood it; on the other was a leather covered bed. A bright fire burned in the grate and on the hob a kettle spluttered out steam.

'Gosh! That's the finest ambulance room I've ever seen,' remarked Jack, 'I'd like to have a good look round in there.'

'You'll get in there quick enough if you're not careful of them ropes,' warned Glyn. There were several notices warning them to 'Beware of Rope Rising'. Altogether there were six different ropes, all pulling from different directions. When a weight comes on the slack ropes they spring up and tighten until they are like a bar of solid steel – and woe betide anyone who gets in the way of that upward swing.

At intervals of eight minutes, 'journeys' of thirty trams full of coal shot out of the drift mouth, to be quickly disconnected from one rope and sent on to their destination by another. Without a second's delay, thirty empty trams rattled inside to replace them. A brook, whose source lay higher up the mountain, came gaily out of the belt of Scotch Fir that crowned the slope into which the drift had been driven. The noise of the machinery drowned the sound of the water as it tumbled past the colliery. It seemed that the poor, frightened brook was trying to steal by unobserved. But it failed – behind a cloud of steam, greedy pumps sucked up water and forced it along to a row of ten Lancashire boilers. Here stokers raked cascades of red-hot cinders from the fire or with one hand directed a hose-stream of cooling water on the cinders and wiped their streaming foreheads with the other. Between anxious glances at the steam gauge they acknowledged the greetings of passing friends .

Farther up the slope a huge compressor was giving a thundering 'oomph-oomph' as it gulped in immense mouthfuls of the morning air and sent them into the engines underground through pipes along which a man could easily crawl. Above another isolated building, a thick smoky spiral smudged the clear sky – foul air from the workings that had been drawn out by the fans. The air and the ground around quivered with the pulse of machinery. Everywhere could be seen the bustle of busy men, shrouded in escaping steam. A stoker stepped across to the side and put one hand on a small lever while the other pulled his watch out of his waistcoat pocket far enough for him to see it. He hesitated, then after a brief pause the lever was pulled and a puff of steam shot up, followed by the blare of the hooter.

'There goes the joy bell,' said one worker, making for the shed where his jacket was hanging. The engines slowed up, the ropes were still for a short while: it was half past six and the night shift had finished. Far inside the darkness of the drift mouth a cluster of tiny lights appeared, rapidly getting closer and bigger until they were made useless by the daylight, and were seen to be the lamps carried by about a hundred and fifty hurrying men. Blinking at the strong light of day, they began a treasure hunt – in cracks in the walls of buildings, under stones and derelict trams, they searched for the pipes and cigarettes they had hidden when they went inside. The nearest stoker threw a newspaper on the low wall, drew a shovelful of red-hot coals from the fire box, and placed it alongside the paper.

'Help yourself, my lads,' he called. They did, ripping strips of paper and lighting them with the coals; then, with their tobacco lit, they thanked him with a wave before moving over to the lamp room. In a very short while they were off the place.

Glyn and Jack crossed to the lamp room. It had five windows, and behind each stood a man waiting to give out lamps. Behind each man were two upright stands, each holding a hundred lamps, every one of them numbered so as to correspond to the number opposite the hook on the stand. About half the lamps were lit, and the five separate windows made a striking sight.

One of the lamp-men noticed the two mates watching by the window.

'Hallo! Are you fresh starters?' he enquired.

'Yes,' replied Glyn.

'Let's see your paper. Thanks. Ah! Colliers, working together. Right! One will have to take an oiler from that top window and here's an electric for you; call for check 356 when you give it back in. He pushed a twelve-pound electric lamp to Glyn; then opened a large book and wrote his name and number in it. Jack got an oil lamp, lighter than Glyn's. These oil lamps are used to detect the presence of gas because an electric lamp will burn where a man will suffocate. A stream of men were getting their lamps and moving towards the drift mouth; Jack and Glyn picked up their tools and joined them. Soon several hundred men had gathered near a notice that read: 'Danger. Cigarettes or matches not to be taken past this spot.'

Glyn let his eyes wander, past the thick green of the fir trees and slowly upwards until above the browning grass of the mountain top he saw a cloudless blue sky that promised a warm day. He looked downward into the drift mouth, where two pairs of narrow gauge rails led to darkness and – what?

Right at his elbow, it seemed, a hooter roared out.

'Time to get in, boys,' warned an official standing by the notice. A group of mining men are always addressed as 'boys' even though some of them may have grown-up sons. Perhaps it is because even after a lifetime of mining work they are still as ignorant as boys to some of the tricks that coal can play upon them. Cigarettes and pipes were hidden, then they moved into the opening. Just a nine-feet circular archway it was – yet every working day for over twenty years two thousand tons of coal had come out through it, though the mountain above showed not a stone displaced as a result.

'Let's help you, mate; I can carry some of them for you, it's a long way,' said a total stranger to Glyn, pointing to the tools. 'And me, too,' said some of the others. In a few minutes the hundreds of twinkling lamps and the men carrying them had gone in and were out of sight. There is nothing alarming in having to walk a long way underground if you are used to it and know that you are fairly safe under the steel arches and brick walls that are used on the main roads. Swinging steel ropes and fast travelling trams are a danger, though much less so if you know about them and take care.

These main ways act as a sort of base line where the enemy – in this case old Craig y Llyn – has been defeated and robbed, and you have strengthened your position. But it is when you attack him on new ground that you must be careful. You are trying to wrest from him something that he does not intend to part with if he can prevent it. He will bring creeping, smothering gas and stifling heat to combat you, will have fatal roof slants and crushing falls of side waiting in ambush. If you persist and drag his treasure out he will fight all the way, leaving deep cuts and poisonous scratches on your body while all the time he is filling your eyes, nose and lungs with a barrage of fine dust. Sometimes he gets really annoyed and lets off his heavy artillery in the shape of a flood; or with a searing explosion gets his own back on a couple of hundred of his torturers – instead of just tinkering around with one or two at a time.

When the crowd of ingoing men had walked for nearly a mile they reached the end of the main road. It split into three sections; the men divided, and followed the roads that led to their working places. At each of these roadways stood a fireman, officials who with practice had learned to blow hard at the glass of the lamp and talk at the same time. Glyn watched all the men as they passed him; hardly one of them carried an ounce of superfluous flesh and all had the pallor that comes from working in unnatural conditions.

Most of the men had moved away and the ones in charge of the traffic had been told how things stood, when an overman came along. A group of boys had dallied behind the others and were arguing. Their eyes were heavy with sleep, and the lamps they carried hit against the rails as if they were too heavy, but their voices were shrill and loud.

'Now, you youngsters,' said the overman coming up behind them unexpectedly, 'you should be in the faces with your butties. Don't let me catch you hanging behind the men again, mind.'

When the surprised boys moved away, the overman noticed Glyn and Jack.

'Oh yes, you're the two new starters aren't you?' he asked. 'Come in here.' He led the way through a doorway into a large underground room. A table with several report books on it stood in the centre; around it were some wooden benches. In one corner was a telephone, watched and listened to by a very busy and excited old man. He would pounce on the receiver before the bell had stopped vibrating, screwing up his face and showing his gums in an effort to hear. Then he would dash out of the cabin, usually colliding with the table, falling over a form, or trying to get through the door before it was opened, in his hurry to get out.

The overman was in no way perturbed. He placed his lamp on the table and his walking stick alongside it, hung his jacket on a hook, rolled up his sleeves and glanced through the reports. That done, he remembered the two who were waiting.

'Oh yes. I suppose I must start you two off. Gwilym – ', the old man swung round, hands on thighs and head thrust forward, 'ring up the Two Feet and ask if they have a place for these two men.'

'They're slow,' snorted Gwilym when the bell had only just stopped ringing. 'I'll – Oh there they are, they are alive.' He spoke into the transmitter, keeping up an emphasis with his hands. 'It's alright, Mr Evans, they're waiting for them,' he finished.

'Right! I'll take you part of the way.' Picking up their lamps, Jack and Glyn followed the official along a sloping roadway where the top was some nine feet above them. After travelling a quarter of a mile the overman signalled them to stop; from above their heads came the sound of voices.

'There's better engine drivers than you in Woolworth's.'

'Well, it's no credit for anybody to say he's an engine driver underground nowadays, what with – '

'It's a lie for you to say it anyhow. If I was you I'd – '

'Latimer!' called the overman. The noise from above stopped at once; then came a whispering the listeners could hear.

'Thought I heard somebody call – sounded like his voice.'

'Can't be him, mun, it's too early.'

'It is him!' answered the official, 'and come on – I want you.'

A man came down the brick steps that led to the engine room overhead. He was a biggish man, middle-aged, wearing an electric lamp on his belt and a doubtful expression on his face. As he neared Glyn noticed a jingling sound, as if the approaching man was wearing spurs. He later discovered that the sound came from a small chain Latimer wore round one of his wrists; attached to the chain was a three-cornered file, used as a signal 'knocker'.

The overman looked at his watch then at the newcomer. Latimer took the hint and moved towards a row of empty trams, jingling the knocker. The overman called to him.

'I want you to take these two down with you to that new skip in the Two Feet.'

'Right,' replied Latimer, 'shove your tools in this last tram and get in that one there. Keep your heads down – and hold tight.'

He drew the file across the double row of signal wires on the side three times; a bell rang three times in the engine house nearby; the sound of moving levers was followed by the roar of released compressed air, then they started to move. Latimer jumped on the coupling between two trams and crouched there, swaying as the speed of the trams rapidly increased. Arches flashed past in one continual blur of steel; lights shone in front of them, blinked, and were away behind. Glyn, sitting on the iron bottom of the tram, was jarred a foot in the air, banged against the sides, and shaken till his teeth chattered. After about ten minutes of this wild flight into darkness they could hear a slackening in the rattle of wheels; Latimer's grip on the tram end loosened, and with a sudden spring he reached the side of the roadway, tucking his body in out of the way of the whirring trams, and knocked the wires. The rope stopped so sharply that the trams jerked back several yards.

'There you are,' remarked Lat, 'we're nearly in the coal face. Of course the others've got to walk down but as you're fresh hands we give you a bit of a treat, like.'

'Thanks,' answered Glyn, wondering how many bones were broken, 'it was alright.'

'It 'ud be better if we had a real driver, one that wasn't afraid to let her go.'

'Yes, it would be better,' agreed Glyn, determined not to give in.

'S'pose I can show you the little dug-out,' Lat continued, taking off his jacket. 'You can take yours off too, you won't want a shirt on when you start to work.'

The heat had been increasing as they went inwards; now it made Glyn gasp, with a dry singeing feeling as if an invisible fire was before them. Lat went into another cabin with a cross on the door; Jack looked in at the hard bed and telephone there, and noted the two stretchers, hung over cupboards that held splints and blankets.

'Interested in ambulance work?' asked Lat.

'Been in the St John's for a long time,' replied Jack.

'That's good; you'll get plenty of practice here,' said Lat cheerfully.

'And four years in the RAMC,[1] added Jack.

'What,' asked Lat, 'was you one of them "rob all my comrades" blokes? Tell you what it is,' he continued, studying Jack's arms and shoulders, 'you're a fool.'

'A fool, why?' asked Jack, mystified.

'For coming in here to work. In the ring you ought to be, a bloke your size. Why, they're paying a man three thousand pounds for a couple of rounds of boxing tonight. They'll give you two bob a ton. Now, I ask you, how many tons will you have to fill to earn three thousand pounds; and how many knock out punches will the mountain give us before we do? Well anyhow, there's the place you've got to work in.'

The 'place' was the edge of a seam of coal about twenty inches thick, into which there was no possibility of Jack getting.

---

[1] Royal Army Medical Corps.

'No,' Lat had seen the difficulty, 'there's no hope of you getting in there, Carnera.[2] Kid Louis[3] here,' motioning to Glyn, 'will have to cut and throw the coal out here. It's not always best to be big, though he's a decent lump.'

Lights farther down the roadway indicated that men were working there. All around, the thud, thud of sharp mandrils being driven to undercut the coal could be heard; then every few minutes came a crashing sound as some of the coal parted from the solid seam and fell, sending out a dense cloud of dust.

They had been busy for about two hours when two men carrying walking sticks and aluminium lamps, the mark of official rank, arrived. 'What are you coughing about,' asked one, 'don't you know that the South dust is the nicest tasting in South Wales?'

'P'raps it is,' replied Jack, 'but you can have it all.'

'Hullo! I thought it was a man I started, not a crane. Don't you go throwing any lumps that size in or you'll break our screens. That's the Horatius that held the path, is it?' asked the other man, the manager. He knelt down to watch Glyn working for a few minutes. 'Yes, you'll do,' he concluded, 'you've been used to the small seams – you didn't learn that trick of swinging the mandril from the elbows in a week. How long were you idle?'

'Six months,' replied Glyn.

'Six months, eh. When things open out a bit we'll give you a chance to make a bit extra to recover lost time.'

Another two hours of slogging, then Lat arrived.

'Come on, my lads; quarter of an hour for grub. I want it too, my belly is sure to be thinking my throat is cut. How about you Carnera? I bet you would like a nice big river to drink, or a sandwich made from a bullock put between two bread carts, washed down with a couple of buckets of broth, eh?'

[2] Primo Carnera (1906–67), 'the Ambling Alp', Italian heavyweight boxing champion of the world 1933–4 and Hollywood film actor. He is reputed to be the heaviest ever world boxing champion.

[3] An ambiguous reference. Coombes is probably alluding to Joe Louis (1914–81), the 'Brown Bomber', world heavyweight boxing champion from 1937 to 1949. He defeated Carnera in New York on 25 June 1935. However, since Louis seems never to have been called 'Kid', Coombes might have had in mind Jackie 'Kid' Berg (1909–41), world junior welterweight champion 1930–1, or even Ted 'Kid' Lewis (1894–1970), world welterweight champion 1915–16 and 1917–19.

'No, I don't feel very much like food,' replied Jack.

Neither did Glyn; after months of idleness both were exhausted by the severe work. They sat back, eyes closed while their companion, quite hardened to the conditions, ate voraciously. Flying dust settled on Lat's food as soon as it was exposed; he washed food and dust down with deep, gurgling draughts of cold tea, all the while keeping up a continual flow of talk.

'Aye. It upsets us all for the first few days, but you'll get used to it. Drink plenty of olive oil and rub it in your arms for the stiffness – that's what I do. The missus says I'll look like oil soon!'

Chapter Five

~

THERE is a rule that colliery companies keep a week's pay 'in hand'. The men are vague as to *whose* hand, but are definite on two points – it is not in *their* hand, neither is a big hand necessary. This arrangement is quite popular when stoppages occur, as then they have a week's pay to draw after they cease work. But it is not at all pleasing when it means working a fortnight before a pay comes, as at the start of a new job. Glyn had survived that waiting fortnight, and, with Jack and Lat, had handed in his slips to the colliery office, receiving in exchange an envelope with a pay inside. The size of the envelope was out of all proportion to the pay; but they had been fortunate to earn a little over the 'minimum' and felt elated as a result.

A handsome girl with a tray of flags stood by the window; she was selling them for the hospital at Galltawe. The monthly deduction of fourpence for that hospital fund was on each man's paper that week, but not one reminded her. Each one hunted in his pay for small change to place in the box, or if only notes were there, was not content until he had shown his mates, and the girl, the bottom of the envelope. She stood in the dust from the screens; her hat, blouse and coat were already spoiled, the cream on her face held the dust into a grey mask.

Outside the gates the ice cream man quickly covered his container after each customer, and a cheap-jack hailed Lat.

'Here y'are' only five bob – real English lever, just the thing for a bloke like you.'

'Will it keep good time?' questioned Lat.

'Good time – why, it'll – '

'Won't slow up at all,' persisted Lat.

'Timed to a second a year,' the salesman assured him.

'Then make that chap in blue overalls buy one. He blows the hooter,' answered Lat, moving away.

'I'll be able to roar to-day,' explained Lat as they went homewards.

'Roar?' asked the puzzled Glyn, 'what d'you mean?'

'You see, when I've got a full week's pay,' explained Lat, 'I goes up to the door, slams it open and marches in. Then I sticks the money on the table and I roars "Hurry up with that dinner, and don't be long with the washing water", but if it's a short week I goes in quietly, and the missus – she does the roaring.'

'What if you haven't any pay coming?' inquired Glyn.

'Then I stands outside the door and chucks my cap in; if she don't chuck it out I creeps in; if she sends it flying out I goes away and comes back to try it later.'

Lat went home to do his 'roaring', which Glyn suspected was nothing like as savage as he made out. Jack took the path for Graig Cottage. Glyn, after passing a large chapel outside which a long queue was waiting to see the relieving officer, entered Line Street, where his home was. Although he had his first pay for many months clenched in his left hand in his trouser pocket, and two pennies, one of them Jack's, to give to the expectant Peter, in the other hand, his cheerfulness left him as he neared his house. Line Street was part of the colliery company's solution to the housing problem. A double row of one hundred and seventy houses, so built that if the wall of one centre house was removed, it was very likely that all of them would fall down. The roadway, which had not had the honour of having been introduced to a steam roller, was an excellent test of sobriety – a drunken man might walk it without stumbling, a sober man never. After dark the houses were a guide to the time one had lived there; long use taught one the exact number of steps that were needed to go down the very poorly lighted pavement before one turned left or right. Strangers with no way of telling one house from the next often entered the wrong house – with various results.

As for the people – how can we point to anyone in Rescwm, or any other town, and say that they are typical? A stranger coming down the street would see Glyn's wife, Jane Owens, seated on the mats she had put on the window sill hours before. He would have noticed her dirty face, untidy hair and slovenly dress; would have seen her hurrying indoors at the appearance of Glyn, for she had suddenly remembered that she had not yet made dinner, and that probably the fire was out. And he would have said – this is a typical miner's wife.

The stranger could not be expected to know that up on the mountain side another miner was sitting down to a plate of steaming dinner, and that he and his mother were talking of their brighter hopes of returning to their native countryside.

The stranger would not know that near Glyn lived Mrs Rowlands, and he would not see her, for she was rarely on the doorstep. Neither was anyone else if she could avoid it, but if he did manage to get into her house he would see Mrs Rowlands dusting the chair before he sat on it and after he got up. Would find her jumping up to wipe a speck of dust off the glittering fender, or to give another polish to the brass rod and row of brass candlesticks on the mantelpiece that steam from the ever-boiling kettle had dulled. When he went out she would follow him to rub the door handle. Probably he would not notice that her front door was varnished and polished. In doing that she had stolen a march on the company – they would not allow her to paint the door the colour she wished, but they could not prevent her making it possible to see her face in it. The outside decoration of these houses was a very simple ceremony; once a year two men arrived with wide brushes and plenty of thin paint. They smeared the doors and window sills green and departed for another year.

Why the company insisted on this yearly greening no one seemed to know; there was better green in plenty on the surrounding mountains. Perhaps it was a belated attempt to replace what they had destroyed, or perhaps it was out of respect to Dr McCarthy. And he deserved their respect, even if his figure and dress were not nearly as imposing as the shabbiest of the many tally-men and insurance men who were at the doors of Line Street. The doctor was coming down the street, a slight jerking figure, always hurrying but never going very fast, the small feet under the flapping grey trousers giving the impression of a cycle rider who has changed down to low gear, but has not yet caught the 'feel' of the pedals.

His figure was often to be seen in the streets about that time on a Friday afternoon; he was mostly in close attention to a large covered lorry that made weekly visits. Its passengers, the 'Bum-bailiffs', were a little more humane when the doctor was watching.

Like African chiefs outside their kraal two men sat on the pavement outside their houses, with the sun glinting on the thick coal dust that covered their faces. They had delayed washing so that everyone in the street should see that they were working, and would have a pay that day. The doctor's jerking feet barely avoided the legs of the talking men and he greeted them without pausing:

'What are ye arguing about, ye varmints? Is it futball? The devil of a lot ye know of it, an'all, you salmon-tin dribblers. Just wait till ye see the Oirish forwards shoving your team into the Channel and back to the home of them agen.' And along the pavement he went with a shuffling run, as if he had a ball at his feet, which was not greatly different from his usual gait.

He reached Glyn's door almost as Glyn himself did; both paused, for they were old friends. The doctor's hands, one holding his stick, went behind his back and eyes that danced wickedly looked up at Glyn from under the bowler hat.

'So ye've started work, I see. Indade an' it's glad I am. Though it's a left-handed thing to say. For if I had my way yr'd not ever go under the ground. Bedad their coal would cost them a pound an ounce before they'd get me to wor-rk it. But it's looking a little stale ye are; ye'd better call at the surgery about closing time for a little tonic.'

'Very quiet with you tonight, doctor,' observed Glyn as he went inside the surgery just after nine that night.

'I pushed them off a bit quick, to have a peaceful hour,' answered the doctor, 'and I've had a few lively ones tonight, an'all. One kid wanted pills for his mother; she'd a bad back, wanted some big pills. "And what for," says I, "do you want big pills for?" "Cos they're better for playing eggs in the nest with in school," he says. And another's been coming pretty often for castor oil and I says "Your dad uses a lot of this oil; does he say it's doin' him good?" "Yes, doctor," he says, "dad says his feet don't get half so sore now." "What's his feet to do with it?" I says, "it's his stomach that's for." "Oh, he uses it to oil his working boots with," says the boy. But come in, you know your chair; I'll lock up.'

They sat inside the consulting room, Glyn in the swivel chair with his back to the writing desk, the doctor on a couch with his feet on the oil stove. They smoked and talked as they had done scores of times together. Suddenly the doctor slid his feet off the stove and got up.

'Was it saying a wasp had stung ye on the tongue, you was?' he inquired.

'Stung me? No,' replied the astonished Glyn.

'Ah! well. Ye never know, ye see. Wasps are very nasty things, and there might be a few of them about. If they want to sting ye, try and get them to sting ye on your tongue, for the spirit in a drop of good whisky is the best antidote I know of, and that's sure. For it's a pity to waste good stuff by rubbing it on the outside, and by the same token, as they say prevention is better than cure, suppose we prevent it now.'

He opened a large case that held a skeleton, and from the back of it brought out a bottle of whisky and two glasses.

'The housekeeper's afraid to look in there,' he explained, 'help yourself. Is that all you take? Double it for me. Sure, it's the best tonic ever invented, better than all the coloured water and weak Lloyd George stuff. What about a little one? You know where it is – I expect it's out of tune.'

'It' proved to be a very ancient fiddle in just as ancient a case, and as the doctor had surmised, it was out of tune. In fact Glyn had never found it anything other than badly out of tune after the doctor had tried to play it. Glyn tuned the A string to the pitch fork, corded and blended the others, played some scales and a few bars of double stopping, then paused to look at the doctor sitting with his head on one side and one eye closed, like a dog that expects to be given a juicy bone. Glyn smiled, took a firmer grip of the chinrest, slid the bow up, and started to play 'Killarney'. The doctor, elbow on couch, watched Glyn's every movement and enjoyed every note. When Glyn changed to 'The Rose of Tralee' he stood up and started to sing along.

'When I won the heart of the Rose of Tralee,' he finished.

It was not good singing, for McCarthy's voice had a way of jumping up and down as if he was singing a duet himself. But the doctor seemed quite pleased with it, and treated himself to another antidote. Glyn refused one.

'That's right, me boy,' said the doctor, 'sure don't let anything delay your playing. Indade, if I could make it sob and sing the way ye can then it's under me arm the ould fiddle would go, and away to the ould country that I'd be at once, and it's meself that doesn't believe that even the Black and Tans would harm me then.'

But 'Mother Machree', usually a favourite, seemed to upset him that night – he sat silent; then brushed his hand across his eyes, got to his feet and replaced the bottle behind a spare shoulder-blade in the cupboard. It was unusual for him to remain so quiet and Glyn wondered whether the music had brought memories of Ireland back, or had recalled that young wife and child whose grave had held him to Rescwm through many years. They parted at ten o'clock, Glyn going home through the rain that was coming down in thick lines like the strokes of a sloping handwriting, hitting the road and splashing up before it swirled to the side and washed the refuse of the streets into the choking drains.

Now there is some idea about that the people of Rescwm are so lacking in either brains or energy, or both, that they cannot organise even a 'penny reading'. It is believed that this idea has been fostered and advertised by the residents of Glynog, a village of like size to Rescwm but built at the top end of Castell Vale some three miles away.

Most people in Rescwm are convinced that it is the success of the Glynog Singing Festival that causes this contempt of their ability. Anyway there is no denying that Glynog's enthusiasts have made it a credit to themselves. Every year at the appointed date lorries carrying a large marquee and several smaller tents arrive in Glynog. In a few hours the football field holds something which from a distance looks like a large white hen sitting in the middle, surrounded by a scattered brood of smaller white tents as chickens. The carpenters of the village made the platform, the electricians laid on the lights, and the others hunted up spare, and used, chairs from the chapels, dance hall and public houses. Then, when the shops had stocked extra supplies and increased their prices, at the same time pushing tables in any odd corner and cards stating 'Teas' and 'Refreshments' in very prominent places, everyone prayed for a fine day. At least, some prayed – and the others merely hoped, or hung on to the fringe of the prayers.

The children competed in the morning session, the adults in the afternoon, and in the evening came the aristocrats – the champion soloists – indifferent to the audience, suspicious of the adjudicators, and contemptuous of one another. This event always took place on a Saturday; and on the next day, Sunday, before the tents were taken down, everyone had a go.

Everyone who could play an instrument got up on the platform and played; the rest crowded into, and outside, the marquee to sing. Everyone who had composed a hymn tune and was present –

and there were several – got up on the platform to conduct it. Everyone who could say a little prayer said it, everyone threw something in the buckets being taken round to collect for the Hospital, and everyone went home sorry that there was only one of those festivals a year.

The strange thing was, although no one from Glynog had become famous in the world of music, Rescwm, with no Festival, had 'turned out' two Doctors of Music. 'Turned out' is the correct term, for in their early struggles their native Rescwm helped them not at all, but rather welcomed their early departure as ridding the village of a disturbing element. Yet when they won the highest position in their profession, Rescwm remembered them and attributed their genius to their being born at Rescwm. Of late Rescwm had not considered it worthwhile to compete at this festival because one adjudicator had actually stated that their choir needed practice badly and had much to learn about singing. Much to learn about singing, mind. To mention the name of that adjudicator in Rescwm afterwards was sufficient to call up memories of a case of colossal ignorance. But Rescwm, too, has its yearly function, one that is far more difficult to arrange than such small affairs as the Glynog Festival. At least this is the definite opinion of most people in Rescwm. I refer to the Annual Sunday School Parade.

This parade occurs every Whit Monday. There are old inhabitants who argue that the parade started first, and that Whit Monday was arranged as a result. As it is rude to argue with age we will leave it at that. Anyway the Parade and the Whitsun holidays were due on the week following Glyn's visit to the doctor. For weeks past the men 'who matter' have been going into one of the chapels on certain evenings. The unusual part is not their going into a place of worship, but that they all go into the same one. They pass through the doors with a troubled glance back at the outside world, then some two hours later they come out again, give one another a faint nod of farewell, and go home. They are the organisers, the keen brains, of those sections in Rescwm who have found the real path to the Celestial regions. Incidentally each of the many sections has a different path, yet each is the only right one. It is only on this occasion during the whole year that they meet – and even then there is something of an armed neutrality about it. In these meetings they pool their knowledge, skill and experience. To decide which is the right path? Tut! How foolish you are – they meet to decide on the route to be taken and other matters concerning the parade. But why all this fuss you will ask, the thing should be simple; just stroll around the place, make sure the children have a good feed, and everyone will be satisfied. Not so – very definitely not so. There is nothing easy about the arrangements for this parade. Rescwm has all the well-known religions and many of the lesser known, and what the latter lack in numbers they make up for in energy.

The first problem is – Who shall lead the march? Shall it be the Church members, the Baptists, the Wesleyans, the Methodists, the Pentecostals, the Independents, the Salvation Army or some of the others? It would have been easy to toss but possibly there would have been objections. When, after long deliberations, they have come to a more or less satisfactory arrangement on that point, problem number two arises. What tunes are to be played?

Now the band have been putting in quite a lot of practice on a new arrangement of 'The Funeral March' and naturally want to play it. The weight of opinion regarding its suitability is against them, however, so they are forced to fall back on 'Colonel Bogey'. An added complication is that each denomination has Welsh and English sections; indeed, some of them have two chapels, one for each language. The Welsh sections want to sing the hymns in their own language because they regard it as being the most musical. In the last parade the first section sang 'Calon Lân'; the next, with no military precision in its step, sang 'Onward Christian Soldiers'; and then came others singing of a green hill far away, when the spectators could see one facing them a quarter of a mile off. Finally the Salvation Army let every one know they were 'Marching to Glory', and had every appearance of getting there, aided as they were by two concertinas and several tambourines.

The route and the music having been arranged, another cause of argument now appears. Which of the national anthems, the Welsh or the English, should be played last? Besides we have Frenchmen who sell us dairy stuffs, and Italians who sell us cigarettes and ice cream. The two first arrivals of these nations – both good fathers and excellent citizens – have been joined by relatives and friends until they form a small colony. They have agreed to the playing of one verse of the 'Marseillaise' as a compromise. A further complication is presented by several 'coloured gentlemen' who in the correct accent are able to answer 'yes' to the question 'Are you from Dixie?' There is a rumour that they intend giving their own musical performance. There is no colour bar in this village and it is thought that this new departure would be enjoyed, for the Dixie-ans have a banjo, guitar, saxophone and some very good voices between them. The treat has not yet materialised though, owing, it is thought, to some doubt as to the proper national anthem of their homeland.

As the day has arrived, and no notification has been given that either Whit Monday or the parade has been postponed, it is safe to assume that all the difficulties have been overcome for another year. Yet there is trouble a-foot, very big trouble – it is raining.

Glyn and Latimer stood in a public house doorway and watched the rain. In Rescwm it is only the public houses that have nice inviting porches in which to shelter from a storm; the places of worship keep you away with rows of railings and high locked gates. Lat was indignant.

'Read this,' he ordered Glyn, holding up a local paper printed the previous Saturday. Glyn read the big headlines – 'Sunshine promised for the holidays. Leave your umbrellas at home.'

'Aye,' commented Lat grimly, 'look at it – raining for two solid days, ever since they printed that paper; leave your umbrellas at home indeed – and take a tin shed with you, I s'pose – huh!'

'That's right,' agreed Glyn, 'these newspaper chaps aren't always right.'

'Never,' replied Lat.

'Oh, I'd hardly say never,' argued Glyn, 'but they often try a bit of bluff on us.'

'Always,' insisted Lat.

But a little while later the rain slackened, and with its easing the hum inside the houses increased until each street resembled an immense hive of bees, awaiting their chance to burst out. A tiny patch of blue sky showed through as the doctor trotted up to Glyn and Lat.

'Is it looking on the black clouds, ye are? Get away with ye, there's enough blue sky to make a triangular bandage now, and sure, there'll be enough to cover the lot of ye before wan hour is gone past.'

True enough – out peeped the sun; and out peeped little faces too, from almost every door. As the streets dried quickly they were filled with children showing each other the new clothes that had meant goodness only knows what sacrifices on their parents' part. Smoke from the rear of the chapels showed that the stokers were getting busy; opened vestry doors allowed alluring views of long trellis tables covered with white cloths, vases of flowers and piles of eatables.

The parade went off fairly well. There was a brave show of banners and the children looked as pretty as children always do. There was, perhaps, some fault on the band, for they made no allowances for the fact that the leading chapel had the oldest inhabitant in front, and it was held to be bad form to precede him in any manner. Consequently, as about one third of the villagers marched and the remainder stood in the doorways to watch their relatives and friends pass by, it was but natural that many should greet the hero who claimed he could easily remember something like eighty of these parades; and he was not rude enough to pass without returning greetings. As a result the band finished about three streets in front of the rest of them, but that had happened before so often that no one took any notice of it. A more serious disaster befell the band; but as whatever happens Glynog must not hear of it, I will tell you only if you promise not to tell them.

It happened this way. Dai Collins, who acts as the scavenger when he feels like it, had decided in view of the heavy rain that morning that he need not collect the ashes. But when the sun appeared Dai suddenly remembered the parade, and judging that full ash buckets would not be very appropriate, decided to do his 'stuff' in a hurry. He managed to finish and was on the way to the 'Dump' when a junction of the streets brought him and the band together.

Dai does not trouble about such trivialities as greasing the wheels of his cart. They were now at the stage when three short squeaks followed one long shrill crescendo squeal. The ash cart turned left, the band right. The big drummer was a small man with a heavy hand, as is usual. He was doing his job very heartily when he noticed the agitated face of the chairman close to his own.

'Old band's playing well today,' called the drummer between thumps, 'specially the cornet. Never 'eard 'im do so well afore.' But the chairman went on gesticulating, finally catching the flailing white arm.

'Leggo you fool,' argued the drummer, 'or I'll lose the beat.'

With difficulty he was persuaded to lower the drum, and by so doing got a good view of the tuneful cart, just in front.

A dumbfounded drummer made his lonely way through the streets to join a drumless and dismal band at the headquarters.

Chapter Six

~

'IT'S a big poster,' commented Tom Brost. It was – something about eight feet high plastered on the end of a house. For in Rescwm the sides of the end houses in the street form part of the main road.

'But wot's the use o' printing a thing like that, when nobody can read the blinkin' thing?' grumbled Tom.

'Can't you read it?' inquired Will Rowlands.

'Tain't likely.'

'Then I will translate it for you,' promised Will. Will had two hobbies – the organ and translating. If someone made a speech in Welsh, he wanted to translate it into English. Then again, if a speech was made in English, Will was not satisfied until he had enlightened someone as to the Welsh meaning of it all. He was an excellent, a gifted, organist, but was far from being so good an interpreter – sentences often got very much altered before Will finished with them. He struggled through the wording of the poster, explaining each word to an impatient Tom. It was the Proclamation, he explained, of the Welsh National Eisteddfod that would take place at Nedd the following Thursday.

'Thought it lasted a week,' interrupted Tom.

'It does,' explained Will, 'the real Eisteddfod, but this is only the Proclamation. The other won't be here until next year.'

'What are they making such a fuss abaht it now for?' asked Tom.

'They want to give them time to get the – the what you calls – ' Will consulted the poster, '*Barddoniaeth* – let's see – what's that in Sais – I mean English. Ah! I know, Poetry – '

'Poultry!' said Tom, brightening up. 'Oh, they've got fowls there.'

'No. Poetry. It's to give time to prepare the essays and poetry.'

'Why can't they print it in English,' complained Tom, as Will continued his task.

'If you'll look at the bottom half you'll see it's in English,' remarked Glyn – and it was. The organisers had forestalled that complaint of Tom's. And he didn't like it.

'Lot of tommy rot, you ask me,' he grumbled, 'we don't bother with things like that up in the big smoke.'

'Don't you? I can remember plenty of processions when I was in hospital there,' argued Glyn.

'Anyhow, you won't ketch me wasting me time there. I kin speak good old English, and that's good enough for me, and it oughter be for the rest of you,' concluded Tom, getting away from Will who was trying to show him which words on the bottom answered the Welsh ones on top.

Will was so fervent that Glyn agreed to go with him to the Proclamation. All the way there he explained what he knew of the old ritual. How the beginning of it was untraced in the past centuries. How it started with just a few who were anxious to sing their songs, recite their poems, and talk of those things which were as the blood of their body, to others who would understand.

'And every year, Glyn *bach*,' he said, 'it is getting bigger and bigger. For this last twenty years I've not missed one that was anywhere near our place. Sometimes me and the missus have had to go short, but she's always found a few bob for me to pay my way in.' Glyn thought of the severe Mrs Rowlands and marvelled. They managed to push their way through the crowds and get to the park where the Proclamation was to be held.

'Men of Harlech march to glory': the notes of the famous national march could be heard clearly, lifting the feet of the procession as they neared the park. A mounted herald came first, then the bands, police and other uniformed men, then the *Urdd*, or Welsh League of Youth, looking very attractive in their green clothes, followed by guides and cadets. Then came the Druids and Bards, each wearing the coloured gown of their particular section. They marched in through the entrance gate between two huge banked-up beds of flowers, and under an archway on which was inscribed in Welsh, *Calon wrth Galon*.

'That means Heart to Heart,' explained Will to all around.

'You see those stones,' continued Will, as the procession circled around thirteen large stones placed in a ring, 'they are to show the counties of Wales. They'll be left there forever, like them up on top of that mountain was, hundreds of years ago.'

By now the park was crowded with people; it was so hot that some were fainting in the crush. A speaker ascended the platform and declared the object of the day, which was to proclaim that the Royal National Eisteddfod of Wales would be held in that town in a twelve-month's time. Then a large crowd of children in Welsh dress sang national airs.

A man in Druid's dress came on the platform; he had a long silver trumpet and played some beautiful music on it, changing his position as he played so that the trumpet was pointing alternately north, south, east and west. The sun glistened on the instrument as he moved round and swayed. Then bard after bard spoke of the objects of the Eisteddfod or recited a poem in its honour. The chief competitions for the following year were announced, a singer sang to the accompaniment of a lady playing a harp, and it all ended with the crowd singing in Welsh 'The Land of My Fathers', as only a Welsh crowd can sing it.

'How do you like it?' asked Will, on the way home.

'Wonderful, very wonderful.' replied Glyn. 'Do you know, Will, I had a sort of awed reverent feeling, like you feel when you stand in a cathedral. Like as if the generations of the past were watching you – I can't explain it.'

'That's how I always feel, Glyn *bach*. Indeed I was hoping that you'd feel that way; that's why I wanted you to come. I'm an old man now; p'raps if I'd tried harder when I was your age I might have got somewhere. I know you're a good musician; why don't you try for one of the big prizes?'

'Are they worth much?'

'Worth much! Not in money – but the honour – the honour! What is money? A man that can make great music, or write a great book, has done something a rich man can never do. A man can make himself rich, but God makes the genius.'

'But look how a working man is handicapped; you should know how our hands are knocked about. Sometimes they're all cuts, and the strings get into the cuts; often I'm too tired to move my fingers and they ache in every joint. You know what things are like at home, you've lived near us long enough; every time I try to practise there's a row. And I should have to compete against others who have every encouragement and help to practise and have never known what it is to dirty their hands.'

'Aye, I know it. But there's no harm in trying. Tell you what – come round with me tomorrow night; it's my practice night on the big organ – yes, that's it – you can come there every week; it'll be one good night's practice for you anyhow.'

And with that understanding they parted.

In the winter Rescwm is a great place for rain; it rains on average six days out of seven. Some people blame the mountains, some the adjacent sea for the continual downpour, and regard as paradises those places that have no rain for years. In past years those villagers who were not welcome in their own homes, such as some lodgers, and some husbands, had no choice but to spend their leisure hours sheltering in shop doorways or under bridges or convenient walls. That is unless they had the inclination and the necessary cash to go into the public houses. There were men in those days who dreamed of a workmen's hall with reading and games rooms, but could see no hope of their dreams being realised until a wise judge decided that one penny off every ton of coal raised should be spent in improving the social side of a miner's life. For that act alone Justice Sankey[1] will always be remembered with gratitude by the miners as one of the greatest benefactors of the colliery districts. Just one penny per ton – not much is it? – but what a boon that levy has been.

As a result, parks and recreation grounds have been made, and libraries built in places where it had been thought impossible. Rescwm had benefited, like many other villages; a fine institute had been built there. It was in this Welfare Institute that Glyn had promised to meet Will – who always miscalled it 'the Farewell'. As he could not see him in the reading room, Glyn settled down to read while he waited for him. But in that he made a mistake, for reading was one of the things 'not done' in that reading room.

---

[1] One of the recommendations of the Coal Industry Commission of 1919, otherwise known as the Sankey Commission after its chair John Sankey (1866–1948), at the time a Judge of the King's Bench, was for a levy on coal to be devoted to welfare purposes such as establishing reading rooms, institutes etc. The Mining Industry Act of 1920 enacted the recommendation and also created the Miners' Welfare Commission to administer the fund.

Had he wanted to know the winner of the two-thirty or why so and so changed his fancy at the last minute, thereby losing the shilling he had borrowed, or if he had wanted to know how much coal this one filled, or timber that one stood, he could easily have had the desired information; in fact it was offered to everyone freely, loudly, and at great length. One group in the corner was almost at blows over Larwood's 'leg theory',[2] because a test match was being played that day. A man on the outside of the group, who had been listening, suddenly inquired:

'Cricket, is it?' The group nodded their agreement. 'Ah!' continued the interrupter, 'who's playing?' And for a brief interval there was an amazed silence in the reading room.

Two newcomers seemed to be taking the view that as a notice on the wall said 'Talking Strictly Prohibited' it was necessary for them to sing. Finally Glyn laid his paper down in disgust and wandered into the much quieter atmosphere of the games room. The fact that one old man, a keen bridge player, insisted on silence while he played and was ready to enforce it with his crutch may have had something to do with the peacefulness there. This room looked rather like a hospital; several had arms in slings, and two pairs of crutches stood against the wall. Two men sat on chairs near the bridge players, men who had been schoolmates together then workmates. Ivor and Fred had been stone, or hard ground, men, who used machines to cut into the rock and came home as white as millers, covered with stone dust. When the strata was too hard for machines they cut holes by delicately turning the steel chisels being driven into the rock by Ivor, who swung a ten pound sledge with deadly accuracy, and for hours at a time. One misplaced blow in the semi-darkness would have meant a smashed hand for Fred and a spoiled borehole. All the time, and with every indrawn breath, stone dust was going into their lungs – and staying there, until the time came when the dust had filled their lungs with a cement-like substance, and every breath became hard work. So hard that their mates had to help them up the few steps that led into the Welfare, where they now spent their days for both

---

[2] Referred to in Australia as 'bodyline', this was a particularly intimidating form of fast bowling which created tremendous controversy during England's cricket tour of Australia in 1932–3. The Nottinghamshire bowler Harold Larwood was its chief practitioner.

had failed to work at the same time. Each thought that he was getting better, but was afraid that the other would never be able to return to work with him.

A group around one of the tables was interested in a large paper plan that lay on it. Will was there; he had a book open and was taking shillings off some of the men and noting down their names.

'I can't understand these blinkin' plans,' complained one, 'I'm not a surveyor, so book me that seat.'

'You can't have that one, Glyn has booked it, and I'm having the next one so's I can have a good seat to watch him play.'

They turned to Glyn, as if expecting to see something different in his appearance.

'Have you entered?' one asked.

'Yes, today,' replied Glyn.

'And if you ask me,' added the organist, 'I think he'll make them go all the way. Have you heard him play lately?'

'No,' replied one, 'but I'll fall in with the rest of you and give my bob a week for a season ticket, instead of going to the pictures.'

'That makes twenty-five reserving weeklies – not bad for a small place, like,' commented Will. 'Come on, Glyn, let's go for that practice.' He folded the plan, placed it inside the book, and followed Glyn across the street to the chapel.

It was a revelation to see Will prepare to play the organ. He would approach it reverently, his eyes tracing each pipe to the high roof, as if he feared one had warped; then he climbed up the steps and sat down before pulling a duster out to wipe the cover – there was no need to dust anywhere for everything in the large building was spotless. After unlocking and raising the lid, he listened carefully until the filling pipes showed that the electricity was doing its work properly. Then he dusted each key separately with a clean handkerchief, and filed his rough finger ends and nails with the striking side of a match box. By the time he had finished this, his invariable custom, Glyn was tuned up and waiting.

'Handel's "Largo",' said Will briefly, pushing a copy to Glyn.

The organ pealed out the introductory bars – then searing an octave higher sang the violin, its rich velvety notes rivalling those of the larger instrument. Will sagged low when the music sank, his chin almost touching his fingers, then half rose in his seat as they lifted to the higher notes. His mouth was wide open in sheer enjoyment, his eyes shone bright. The last quiver of music had passed over the galleries before he turned to Glyn, rubbing his hands together.

'Good! Yes, indeed, very, very, good. I'd like to play it again and again but there'll be plenty more chances won't there? We will try something else – there's a pile of music in that cupboard,' he pointed, 'take the solos out, and hand me the piano parts, I'll manage with them.'

Two hours had jumped by, and dusk had come. The shaded electric lights in the organ corner gleamed on polished woodwork, on ivory white keys, on grey pipes that went up to the darkness of the roof, and on the seated figure of Will. Eyes intent on the music page, fingers rippling along the notes and sometimes flashing sideways to alter a stop, his body swaying with the movement of his feet changing pedals – he was master, yet slave, of the organ. Near him stood Glyn, straight and almost motionless of body, fingertips dancing on the strings or holding them to a sustained vibrato, a supple wrist controlling the bow.

At last Will stopped and slowly pulled the cover over.

'I s'pose we must pack up,' he said regretfully, 'or the caretaker will be grumbling.' He started to put the music away, then jumped as a dry, rasping cough sounded from near the doorway. Glyn turned – he knew that cough. In the half light near the door sat Fred and Ivor. By some great effort they had struggled there. 'Been – here – a – long – time – ,' gasped Fred. ' 'Twas – great. – Tried – not – to – make – row – by – coughing – and – stop – you. Ain't – been i – in – one – of – these – places – sin – since – was – a – little – 'un.'

They helped him home, and Ivor confided in Glyn that he would be working again before very long; he was afraid Fred wouldn't get better, and it would be lonely without him as they had always been together. They were together to the end, dying in the same week, hardly a month later.

Jack, always so generous with his help and sympathy, was usually very sparing with words. But Glyn's decision to compete at the National made him quite excited and delighted. Difficulties? Puff! He waved them away. Damaged fingers? He'd watch that – from now he was going to handle all the stones; Glyn was to do the jobs that wouldn't hurt his hands. He, Jack, was strong enough, and he could help others, why on earth shouldn't Glyn let him do it? No place to practise? Why not come every night to their place at Graig Cottage? It was quiet enough there and his mother wouldn't mind. But Glyn would not allow that. If he could not do it in his own home then he was not going to be a nuisance to others. They spent some time arguing in search of a solution, but at last found a place that suited well.

Chapter Seven

~

DOCTOR McCarthy slowly replaced his hat, and watched the figure of Myfanwy Darrell as she climbed upwards, disdaining the help of the white railings. Pausing at the first turn she took off her hat, giving the mountain breeze a chance, which it took, to frolic with the thick brown hair. Then she raised one bare arm, hardly different in colour from her white silk blouse, in answer to the watcher's salute, before continuing the climb.

'Sure, an' it's the grand walk she's got,' muttered the doctor as he turned away, 'walking up that hill the same as a soldier, and an Irish Guardsman at that. An' the skin of her – like the cream in me mother's dairy; it's a colleen she is, and that's sure. Devil a one of them flat-footed, standoffish, English women but would faint at the need to climb there; and she goes up it like a bir-rd, entire-ly.'

The roadway to the Graig Cottage from Rescwm is too hard for even the stout hearts of the roadmen. As nature has built a road there, man can leave it alone. Motor cars have never climbed it – probably they never will. On the few occasions that wheeled carts, lightly loaded but drawn by three slipping, straining horses, have surmounted it victory has remained with the road. The solid rock flooring showed no mark of the journey; the cart wheels had scars in plenty.

The road, twisting to make climbing easier, became much more level after passing the turn at the end of the white railings. Here Myfanwy stood to recover her breath and look back at the valley. A shimmering blue heat haze, like a mirrored wave, spread across it. The sound of a steamer's siren came through the haze; the shouts of hawkers – the sound of a motor horn – came upwards from that muddle of grey houses and streets that was Rescwm. But apart from that grey blotch the valley was an emerald green, deepening where the trees on Hir Fynydd, the opposite mountain, met the bottom fields. Here and there on the mountain side were small clearings, circling what looked like splashes of whitewash but in reality were small farmhouses. Myfanwy's eyes lingered on these then dropped as something moved below. A train of loaded coal trucks was moving out slowly from the colliery sidings. The engine driver was allowing the slight gradient to take them along, making it appear that the trucks were pushing the engine, and that it was too hot for the engine even to puff out smoke. She could just distinguish the name on the trucks. When she was in London her eyes had often looked out for trucks with that name, as a link to her valley home. She remembered seeing one in a siding and getting up close to touch its dusty sides, wondering if in among those tons of coal it held was one lump cut by brother Jack – or perhaps Glyn. A whiffle of wind lifted dust off the trucks below her and blew it over the lines of washing. Myfanwy turned, passed the corner, and seemed to be in another world.

Waist-high ferns filled the spaces between the trees and encroached until the road became a path; from among them came the whirr of grass-hoppers, sounding like miniature mowing machines. The great mountain stretched across and upwards until it seemed to meet the blue sky. The roadway had been winding alongside a deep gorge, at the bottom of which ran a small river. This river, the Graig Avon, started up in the mountain and rushed downwards, until just in front of the Darrell's cottage it was held up by slabs of flat rock which the running water had washed clean, as if they were the doorsteps of an immense house. Then some little distance farther down it tumbled into the gorge eighty feet deep, with a roar that could always be heard at the Darrell's home.

Myfanwy had reached the point where she could see the upper part of the fall frothing downwards when she caught the sound of music rising above the noise of the water. The notes of a violin, exquisitely played, went throbbing across the deep cleft and were thrown back by the rocks and trees on the other side. All the time the rushing cataract kept up a dream-like accompaniment, in the same way as air does when it is escaping from a bag pipe.

'Oh! How lovely,' she gasped, in sheer pleasure; then moving carefully along the edge she peeped over. From there she could see the player standing on a grass patch the size of a small garden. Spray from the falling water was reaching the edge of this green space, and on the cliff side she noticed a small, neatly built shelter with a reed-thatched roof. Unseen herself, she watched and listened for a while then turned and made her way across to the cottage.

The scent of the lavender bushes came to meet her and mingled with the smell of newly split oak as she opened the gate. A white standard rose faced a dark red Hugh Dickson across the cobbled path; both bowed slightly as she passed; the busy wind, deeming perhaps that it had been rude long enough, shook the cluster roses on the trellis arch, and greeted her with a scented shower of petals. The new lime wash on the walls smelled sweet and fresh, as did the faint odour of carbolic soap inside the kitchen. In the pantry was a small churn and milk tins, polished and waiting. In the kitchen the old grey cat slept with her paw over a kitten that Myfanwy had not seen before. The cat opened her eyes to the strange touch, then went to sleep again. In the parlour a photograph of Myfanwy in nursing uniform stood on the well-polished top of the piano.

Out again into the garden, where the currants were hanging thick, the beans almost to the top of the poles, and the nasturtiums climbing over Jack's rustic summer house – but there was no sign of her mother. She was not fetching water, for Myfanwy could see the small pipe from which ran the spring water. She walked around the lower end of the wall – and saw her mother seated on a stone, a small chick in one hand; and in the other a thin feather which she was pushing down the chick's throat and turning. An agitated mother hen was clucking and fussing about while the rest of her brood watched the performance from a safe distance, and an Airedale dog held a sort of watching brief over the lot.

'Mother,' called Myfanwy, softly.

Mrs Darrell sat up, but did not turn at once. Her face had the look of one that was dreaming; the chick dropped from her slackening hand and lost no time in joining its family and disappearing in the ferns; the dog turned round slowly then made a sudden, noiseless rush, almost knocking Myfanwy over with his welcome.

'Myfanwy,' said the mother, her eyes big with surprise, 'but is it you indeed, *merchi*?'[1]

---

[1] A Welsh colloquial form meaning 'my girl'. It can also mean 'my daughter'.

'Indeed it is, mother.' Grey eyes looked fondly into other steady grey eyes, brown hair that trapped the sunlight mingled with greying hair, and satin-like cheek touched skin roughened by sun, wind and age. The dog sat panting, its tongue hanging, conscious of having done his share.

'But *merchi*, why didn't you let me know you were coming?' asked the mother, holding her at arm's length after the first embrace and scanning her face anxiously. 'And dear, dear; how pale you look; that old hospital has stolen all your colour.'

'And have you slaving to make a lot of preparations, and running up and down to the station to meet me! No, mother; this is how I like to find you, doing the things as I remember you, as I've pictured you doing them every day.'

'You didn't say anything about your holiday being due in your last letter.'

'I didn't want to disappoint you, because I wasn't sure. I saw there was a vacancy for a staff nurse at Galltawe. I told Matron, she recommended me, but said that if I didn't get the appointment, I was to stay on. Only yesterday I heard I'd got it; so here I am, and I'm going to have a week's holiday before I start.'

'Galltawe! Why that's only about twelve miles away isn't it?'

'Yes, I'll be able to see you every week. What do you think of that, mother, a day at home with you every week?'

'You know how very glad I am. I felt anxious about you lately; I was thinking of you just before you came.'

'The thought of that operation you were going to do, I suppose. I see it's not only in hospital that they have operations. I should think that the chick is grateful to me for coming.'

'They've got gape worms in their throats. But come in the house; where's your cases?'

'I left them at the station. Perhaps Jack will fetch them for me.'

'He won't be long doing that when he knows you've come; but he's out somewhere – I expect he's with Glyn for they're always together.'

'No he isn't. I saw Glyn playing by the falls as I came up – he's playing splendidly now.'

'He goes there and practises for hours each day; they built a shelter in case it rains; he spends most of his spare time there.'

'But why does he always go there to practise?'

'He never says straight out, but I can guess. He comes there for peace, and I'm sure I don't blame him. Uch! that woman! It makes my heart ache when I see how miserable his life is; and it would take so little to make him happy. Dear *annwyl*[2] – that's how it often is in life, a good man and a poor woman, or – But look at me, talking and haven't even put the kettle on yet.'

'Shall I make tea, mother?'

'No, indeed you won't! You sit down.'

'I'm not in a great hurry. Perhaps Jack will be back in half-an-hour; so I'll stroll down and see how Glyn is getting on.'

'Well, bring him back with you to tea, *merchi*, and don't be longer than half-an-hour.'

Myfanwy walked back towards the falls, going slowly; drinking in the keen mountain air, entranced by the peaceful freshness all around. As she approached the gorge she made her way quietly and, as she thought, unobserved, getting closer to Glyn who, with his music stand under a tree branch, was playing wholeheartedly, oblivious to anything else. Step by step she went nearer until, when only two yards from Glyn, she came level with the shelter.

Suddenly a small head, with a mop of brown curls that crowned a freckled face and dancing eyes, peeped out of the shelter. A toy pistol and a wooden dagger were pushed inside a piece of string tied around the small boy's waist.

Myfanwy stopped in pretended fear as a strained bow and arrow was pointed towards her.

'Peter! You little imp, how you've startled me.' She caught him under the armpits and swung him up level with her face. 'My word! You have grown – and what are you playing at now?'

'Indians,' replied Peter pointing to the shelter, 'and there's wolves an' all up there,' pointing to the towering rocks on the other side.

'And you, Paganini – haven't you anything to say?' she asked the astonished Glyn, who seemed to have lost the power of speech in his surprise. He was the only one she seemed to like to tease, and the name for the great violinist was her favourite nickname for him.

'Why – I – I didn't even know that you were coming home. Jack didn't tell me,' he complained.

[2] The Welsh word for 'dear'. The expression is a colloquial one, the equivalent of 'Dear, dear'.

'You could hardly expect him to – when he didn't know himself. But what are you practising so earnestly at – that you do not notice my coming?'

'It's the test piece for the next National, Myfanwy. I only got it this morning; I – I thought of trying. You see there's a long time before it comes off.'

'Don't let me delay you. Go on – play for Peter and me, and we'll sit down and keep ever so quiet; because if you're both very good I'm to take both of you back with me for tea.'

'Indeed, Glyn,' remarked Myfanwy, half-an-hour later as they were crossing to the cottage, 'I think you are quite justified in trying. I have heard players made a fuss of in London that were not as good as you – in playing I mean. If a humble accompanist is any use to you, I shall be home every week from now on, and can help in that way.' Then she told her news.

'Things certainly seem to be running my way,' said Glyn, elated, 'what with you and Will Rowlands – he makes me go with him one night a week.'

'Is he still as good as an Englishman as ever?' inquired Myfanwy, 'Poor old Mr Rowlands, I've often laughed at his sayings.'

'Just about the same. He told me last week that any improvement in my playing would make it worse.'

'His way of saying that it couldn't be bettered, I suppose.'

'He told me that the old gentleman that lives at Derwyn House was the one that could help me. He said that he'd got a lot of influence in things like that. I think he was a composer once or something.'

'Why don't you go and see him then?'

'It's easy to say, isn't it? But everyone around here knows he doesn't welcome visitors. Will wasn't anxious to come with me even.'

'Jack told me you were a splendid soldier,' said the Myfanwy, smiling, 'yet you're afraid of an old man who is a cripple. Indeed I'm surprised we won that war.'

Tea at the Graig Cottage that night was a meal of cheerful talk and recalled memories. Afterwards the piano awoke from a long silence. Jack and his mother sat on each side of the fireplace listening to the airs of their native land being played by two whose fingers moved in perfect unison. Peter divided his attention between a large stick of candy and the music. After greatly enjoying both, and getting very sticky, he fell asleep on the mat in front of the fire and had to be carried home.

'We're both in good practice now, Glyn,' said Myfanwy, four nights later, 'and before my holiday is finished I've promised to take you to see Mr Johnnes.'

'Mr Johnnes – of Derwyn House?' asked Glyn incredulously.

'Yes. Why not? You look as if he was an ogre.'

'How do you come to know him so well? They say he doesn't allow anyone there but the servants.'

'He doesn't as a rule. But I nursed him through a serious illness, and he found out we came from near Aberystwyth. In fact he used to live not more than a mile from our old home. He has a very fine house there now. Since then, he insists that I go and see him every time I am home.'

'I heard he was a great composer once.'

'And a conductor too. Oh, yes, he'll pick out your faults! He seems quite anxious to see you – I told him that I knew a first class violinist here and would like to introduce him. He was surprised and said he would be pleased to see you. Now remember, I've told him we'll be there tomorrow night so don't forget or run away.'

But it was a very dubious Glyn that accompanied Myfanwy to Derwyn House the next night. The way from the cottage was along a roadway that crossed a bridge at the top of the falls, then wound down towards the valley. On each side were high walls of thick flat stones laid together without any mortar. These walls are as solid as they were when built, centuries before; they act as boundaries and in some places run almost to the top of the mountain.

After some distance the surroundings became less rugged, and they came down through a wood of oak and ash trees, behind Derwyn House. The house was built in a *pant*, or hollow in the mountain. The sides and back were sheltered, and shadowed by the wooded mountain sides; but in front the sloping ground allowed a clear view of the valley. It looked immensely strong with its yard-thick stone walls – and if tales were to be believed, it had secret passages and dungeons, which had been used when famous warriors in the area's history lived there.

'Mr Johnnes is expecting you,' said the maid who answered the bell, 'will you wait in the music room, please?'

Mr Johnnes was reputed to be a rich man, and Myfanwy had said he was a music lover. Certainly the room seemed to confirm these opinions, for it was laid out solely, and without stint, for the enjoyment of music. A splendid grand piano and a carved music stand stood in the centre, and there were shelves holding music all on one side. An electric cluster lamp threw light on the piano and stand, and was shaded in such a way that the rest of the room seemed steeped in a dark red shadow. Glyn, surprised by the unusual sight of luxury, let his eyes search the room until he noticed, on the right side of the door, a glass case displaying eight different violins. His gaze went no farther; he bent and examined them – even at first sight he knew that he was looking at instruments that were not of ordinary make. The room and the house were strangely silent, so quiet that when Myfanwy turned a page of music it made a loud disturbing noise.

Glyn, entranced by the contents of the case, started as her voice broke in. 'Mr Johnnes – this is Glyn Owens.' Turning, he saw an elderly, bearded man in an invalid chair wheeling himself into the room.

'So you are the Glyn of whom our mutual friend has told me so much,' was the greeting of the elderly gentleman; but Glyn noticed as he shook hands that although the body in the chair did not move, the hands were restless and strong, and quick, keen eyes were searching his face. 'I noticed you were interested in my treasures, Mr Owens. I had been led to expect that of you. Would you mind handing them to me?'

Glyn carefully opened the glass door, and handed the first to him with the question:

'Isn't this an Amati model,[3] Mr Johnnes?'

The elder man's eyebrows went upwards, a pleased smile lightening his features. 'Ah! So you have some knowledge of the old makers; this is indeed a surprise. May I enquire if you have studied them deeply?'

'Hardly deeply, for I have only been able to study the methods from some old books I came across; but I was so interested that I have remembered almost every one of the main points.'

---

[3] The Amati were an Italian family of violin-makers at Cremona during the sixteenth and seventeenth centuries.

'It is a genuine Amati. I am sure you will be pleased if I explain in detail. You'll notice the shallow sides and almost flat front – it is built that way to give sweetness of tone. If you will hand me the next one – thank you – you will notice that it has a higher front and is deeper in the sides; consequently it has a much more robust tone. Yes it is a Guarneri.[4] The other six are my own make. I have tried to copy the best features of the old makers and add some improvements of my own. I have sent for the best fifty-year-old pine in Italy for the fronts and bird's eye maple for the backs, and I have worked them down to the thickness of a threepenny bit.'

'Yes, I realise it must be very delicate work – one slip would destroy weeks of effort,' agreed Glyn.

'Will you believe me, Mr Owens, when I tell you that each one of these instruments has cost me three months' hard work, that is as hard as a man in my condition can work.'

He paused and looked keenly at Glyn, and after a short silence asked:

'Why do you not ask me the usual question – how much do I expect to get for them?'

'I should never have asked that. Because to me there's no question of value or payment. They are yours – you have made them yourself – what money can buy a treasure like that?'

The elder man did not answer immediately; when he did, his voice sounded husky.

'Perhaps you would like to see my workshop? Will you excuse us for just a little while, Miss Darrell? There is plenty of music if you care to play while we are away.'

He led the way, wheeling himself quite easily to the room he had fitted up as a workshop. In it were tiny vices, scales for weighing the sections of the models, moulds in which to clamp them, and pieces of wood already partly cut out.

'You chisel the back and front out of the solid piece, do you?' inquired Glyn.

'Yes. It is only the cheap factory makes that are pressed to shape,' replied the other.

---

[4] The Guarneri were also an Italian family of violin-makers, based in Cremona, Mantua and Venice during the seventeenth and eighteenth centuries.

Wonderfully small tools, like a watchmaker's, were on the table. Nearby was a block of wood partly sawn.

'I am sawing that out of the rough at present. At one time I had them sawn for me, and invariably they were spoiled. Now I do it myself, although it is slow work. But I never hurry – time is nothing to the desire of making a first-class instrument. If sawn the wrong way it is useless – it must be sawn so as to get the smaller grain in the centre.'

Glyn had his hand on the saw.

'May I?' he asked, and when the other nodded he sawed steadily, and in a few minutes finished it.

'There,' said Mr Johnnes, smiling; 'you have completed my task for tomorrow. But let us get back to Miss Darrell – we can explore the workshop more fully some other day.'

The sound of the piano came out to them as they were going back. Glyn stood as his host held up a hand – they both listened. The elder man nodded.

'The "Prelude" – quite a difficult piece too; but she has a wonderful touch, that girl. Both in healing and music – and they run together very well those two – very well indeed. Yes, music itself does a deal of healing, that I know from experience. The mystery is how she can find time to practise – as she most obviously has – while working such long hours. But when the heart craves, obstacles can be overcome – witness my own feeble efforts and your own struggles – of which Miss Darrell has fully informed me. Ah!' he gripped his hands together, 'that girl plays with her heart, and the piano becomes a living thing. I have allowed no one, with the exception of Miss Darrell, to play that piano since my wife – ' he checked himself abruptly, ' – shall we go in?'

'Mr Owens has completed my work for tomorrow in ten minutes,' he told Myfanwy, laughingly, 'but I hope you will forgive us for leaving you so long alone. When we men start on our hobbies we forget all else – but you must be impatient for some music, Mr Owens – will you favour me by playing one I have made? I am anxious to hear what the tone is like – I will be the audience.' He wheeled himself near the big open hearth, in which a newly-lit log fire was crackling. They played selection after selection, solos and overtures. Glyn, although delighted with the first violin, changed his instrument at the wish of the elder man, until he had played them all. For most of the time the listener sat without speaking, his hands keeping an unconscious beat, his eyes fixed on visions in the fire. After the fifth piece he held out his hand –

'May I see the pianoforte copy?'

'There's no need,' laughed Myfanwy, 'I know I lost the time about half way through; but Glyn kept on and we came together again. Perhaps I was a little nervous – a little afraid of our audience.'

'There is no need for either of you to fear any audience, in fact you had played so well that I thought the copy might be wrong.'

Occasionally he would remark:

'I think the tone of that one is quite equal to the Guarneri,' or 'that one has the fine flutey tone that is so much admired,' but as a rule only a satisfied nod of reward came from the figure in the red shadows. The pleasant hours sped by unnoticed until the house-keeper brought coffee and biscuits.

'May I thank the two of you for a wonderful evening,' said Mr Johnnes, and turned to Myfanwy. 'Your Glyn has fulfilled all your promises. Indeed I was astonished at the way he played; and the tone he brought out of my instruments – it is the first time I have heard them played. I never dreamed there was a player like him so close to me. Before you go will you play me Beethoven's "Adieu" – it is a piece of which I am very fond; and be very sure that I shall look forward to seeing either or both of you as often as you can come.'

They played Beethoven's haunting melody – then walked together, through the moonlight, past the falls – and home.

'Why are you so quiet, Paganini?' teased Myfanwy. 'Haven't you enjoyed the evening?'

'Enjoyed it! That's what's the matter. I've enjoyed it too much. I have seen how happy we could be if only we had a chance. When I'm very happy or very sad I can't find the words to express it. But tonight I could play my feelings to you.'

Myfanwy went to her new duties and left an empty place at Graig Cottage, but gradually Glyn became a frequent and very welcome visitor at Derwyn House. A close friendship developed between the crippled gentleman and the young vigorous work-man, both drawn together by their mutual love of music.

Mr Johnnes had found a friend who delighted in doing the rougher parts of the work, leaving the delicate parts and the finishing to the master, and could give glorious voice to his hitherto silent creations. Glyn found his eyes opened to a new life, and that the elder man could give him the technical advice he so badly needed, such as 'I think it would be an improvement if that opening movement was played more softly' or 'I would prefer more nip in that staccato run.' As the months went past Glyn found, too, that some influence was at work making his services in demand at concerts and musical festivals, sometimes at a distance from the valley.

Then followed busy evenings of practice, and visits to Derwyn House, watching, and helping Mr Johnnes while he chiselled front and back from the solid blocks of wood, bent the sides and united them in the mould. Then came the eager wait for the glue to fix before the all-important test, and Mr Johnnes would wheel himself to the other end of the hall so that he should know how the new violin sounded from a distance.

He had composed a piece of music in memory of his wife, and showed Glyn how to add the accompaniment to the solo, and the rules of melody in adding thirds, fifths and octaves. When the arrangement was completed he laid it regretfully to one side: 'We must leave it until Miss Darrell comes again; then we can try it over to hear how it sounds.'

Glyn had been curious for some time as to the total absence of other visitors, and remarked:

'But you could get some other pianist to try it out for you.'

Then he saw a different man to the quiet, ever polite one he had hitherto known. His eyes flashed – the reply stabbed out –

'Yes! And have them trying to teach me my business in the first half-hour. Bah! I am sick of these Welshmen around these parts . . .'

Note:

The final page of this chapter is incomplete. During the course of the subsequent chapters, 'Castell Vale' traces the continuing romance of Glyn and Myfanwy, and their increasing involvement in the life of Mr Johnnes. At the end of the novel the death of Glyn's wife enables Myfanwy and him to marry and live with Mr Johnnes in the old house he owns in rural Cardiganshire, near the Darrells' original home. Both face, and surmount, great tribulations along the way, including the deaths of some of the major characters: Jack, Mrs Darrell, and Glyn's son, Peter (though no clues as to the circumstances of the latter have survived). Glyn succeeds in qualifying for the final round of the violin competition at the Eisteddfod but does not win it, probably because of the serious events that occurred the previous evening. During the night shift underground, while his mother lies unconscious in hospital, Jack is killed, probably as a result of negligence on the part of a mine official. The two leading characters' ties with Castell Vale are thus inexorably cut, enabling them to set up a new life together and to pursue, with Mr Johnnes, their love of music.

THE WAR DIARY OF
A WELSH MINER

INTRODUCTION

'The War Diary of a Welsh Miner' is a record, compiled approximately on a weekly basis, of Bert Coombes's reactions to the first
seventy-two weeks of the Second World War. Whether the idea
behind this was Coombes's own, or whether it was suggested to
him, is unclear, although in a letter written to Gwyn Jones in
January 1941 he mentioned that Gollancz had 'taken an interest'
in the venture.

The 'rough draft', as it is labelled, was completed up to January
1941. It seems then to have been sent to World Press Features
Ltd. of London, but no more is known as to any response it
received. Coombes would not, in any case, have wasted too much
time worrying about its fate, as he was entering one of the busiest
periods of his writing career, writing another two books, many
articles and even film scripts before the end of 1945. As for his
weekly contributions to the *Neath Guardian* (1940–1, 1944–5)
there is little overlap between the 'War Diary' and his newspaper
articles, although it is possible that the effort he had expended in
compiling the former rendered the labour of the latter rather less
onerous.

The 'War Diary' runs to over thirty thousand words, twenty
thousand of which are published here. Although there is nothing
to suggest that it was not written on a weekly basis, Coombes
provides no regular dates, and his practice of consecutively num-
bering the weeks is sufficiently inconsistent to make the precise
identification of each week an impossibility. Where there are clues
(in the form usually of reference to external events), footnotes
have been inserted to provide corroborative information. The
entries for a few weeks have been deleted, as being of no consequence, and those for others have been shortened, but every
effort has been taken to ensure that the balance of the 'War Diary'
and the representativeness of its content have not suffered as a
result.

The War Diary of a Welsh Miner

~

SO we are at war. We have been cowards in the past, scarcely caring who suffered as long as we avoided the danger. In this area we miners contributed our coppers every week to help the Spanish Government and held demonstrations and meetings appealing in aid of them because we realised that they fought our battle. Apart from the Communist section the only political party in this area – and for many miles around – is the Labour Party. I do not know one who professes to be a Conservative and only just a few are Liberals. So in order to get the views of other parties and people I go to the miners' welfare library every night and read the *Times, Daily Telegraph* and *Western Mail*. Over Spain it seemed that even these papers could not plead with confidence for their leaders and to us it seemed that the wishes of the whole Principality were ignored.

The betrayal of the Czechs hit us like a blow in the face. We counted them as our ally, a well-governed, well-equipped friend. No wonder that 'to do a Runciman' is the new term for shady work.[1]

Yet we are to fight for Poland, a country that is farther away from the mind and knowledge of most of us. Recently I was reading an article by a traveller through Poland. He said that the peasants lived in terrible hovels, but that the nobles had carpets along the walking ways to their stables. Also that each great family had its special waiting room at the local station, only to be opened

---

[1] Lord Runciman was sent to Prague as a mediator in July 1938 and on his return recommended self-determination for the German population of Czechoslovakia, thus paving the way for the Munich Agreement of September 1938.

when they needed its shelter, but that ordinary people had not the least protection from the weather.

The first official mention of the declaration of war came to us over the wireless and spoiled my taste for a nice dinner.[2] I think they had changed the transmitting length suddenly as we had a job to get a reception for a while. Then we heard the voice of the announcer speaking slowly 'A state of war now exists . . .' His voice stopped abruptly and over the air there sounded an enraged voice rushing out angry and guttural words – German we thought. After some seconds everything was silent; several minutes passed before the British announcer resumed. Reception was bad for many days. Later we heard Chamberlain explaining the situation; a tame and dreary speaker.[3]

~

A week has passed and nothing much happened here. We are surprised at the placidity of this war. We are told that Poland is well-equipped and will hold the enemy for months. The news is that the Poles are advancing in some sectors. Still no sign of enemy planes or news of mass attacks on our towns. The blackout does not worry us much in this house because we are outside the area of street lighting and it was always dark at night once we got past the range of our house lamps. We have barred and shuttered windows. When dusk comes we close the shutters and our blackout is complete. I wonder, did the men who built this house and placed the shutters as a protection from the highwaymen ever guess that they would be used as a shield against an invader from the skies?

~

Another week, surprisingly uneventful. We had expected there would be no London by now and we were not alone in that fear, to judge by the way that businesses and big institutions have moved out. We have to send everything to new and strange addresses.

[2] Britain declared war on Germany on 3 September 1939.
[3] Neville Chamberlain, Conservative Prime Minister from 28 May 1937 to 10 May 1940.

Insurance forms and National Health papers have to be sent in fresh directions. Already some of the shops are pleading scarcity as an excuse for rising prices.

I think the blackout on car lights makes the road pleasanter for walkers. We used to stumble along homewards in a blinding continuity of light before the war; now the dimmed lights are easier on the eyes and of course, the cars are fewer. It is very difficult to find an isolated house alongside the road now and we get out of the buses many yards away from the desired spot. Our old custom was to leave the door and windows open in such a way that the light could be seen from the road as a guide to the returning traveller – that is forbidden now and we peer out from darkened bus windows trying to note some stretch of road that will guide us; often I have gone by the swing of the bus when it rounds a turn a hundred yards away. When we are set down it is necessary to stand for awhile until our exact position is defined. The dogs are useful as a guide when they rush out to greet us. Several times I have walked into a wall or fallen over a curbstone. Torch batteries are not to be had here.

~

This week it is obvious that Poland has been completely beaten, that the Germans have advanced so fast that little opposition could have been offered. Also that the Polish leaders have led their people swiftly and definitely – in the retreat. Why did Poland collapse so easily? We were told they were perfectly equipped and trained yet they were brushed aside – with the exception of Warsaw – as if manœuvres were taking place. Yet the Spanish people, unarmed and untrained, resisted for years. Was it the leadership or the cause?[4]

~

My ambulance experience and training look like coming in useful. I have received a form in which it states I am to do 'continuous duty at the Resolven First Aid Post' . . . 'Duty with the Mobile

---

[4] Warsaw fell to the Germans on 27 September, and the following day Poland was partitioned between Germany and the USSR.

First-Aid Party' . . . 'Travel with ambulance car through Neath and District' etc. Not all at the same time I hope.

To clear up the situation I have offered to take charge of the ambulance hall every Saturday night as it is the only night when I am not in work – and some of the other members who work days are often on duty by night as well. This arrangement will give them a week-end break.

We had a fine example of official stupidity during this last week. The coal is being tipped on both shifts so that the afternoon men had the latter part of their working period after dark. The rider who conveyed the trams from the drift mouth to the screens was not allowed to have a light of any sort and it was impossible for him to fix ropes and couplings in the dark, so the shift had to stop. Four hundred men were kept idle and about six hundred tons of badly-needed coal was lost each afternoon. Scores of pleasure cars were passing our house each night, every one carried more light than our rider needed, but it did not matter, he must work in the dark or not work at all, so the shift had to finish. I am one of the Federation committee-men and we are confident that it is a case of some local authority getting too important for his size.[5] We are going to send a deputation to the Ministry of Mines.

~

Winter, a dark and grey season, is closing round us. The hedges are bright brown and the bracken on the mountain sides has gone a rusty colour. The leaves are falling all around us and when we open the back door they rush inside as if seeking warmth. Our deputation has been successful; it was a ridiculous position anyway. The journey rider is now allowed to carry an electric cap lamp which he can switch off instantly and gives about as much light as a good torch. So now the men are all back at work. They have lost more than a week and some five thousand tons of valuable coal have not been mined. Someone would have had a sharp kick in the pants if I had been Minister of Mines.

~

---

[5] 'Federation' refers to the South Wales Miners' Federation.

As this place is isolated from the rest of the village we depend a lot on the wireless for our amusement – and for the news of course. To me the BBC seems completely demoralised. Their programmes are doleful and the majority of the speakers are as dreary as a chapel secretary who knows that the collection will not be more than half-a-crown. There is general complaint about the dullness of the programmes and yet one can switch over to a continental station and get sparkling music and blithe programmes. The Thin Red Line – what a selection for times like these.[6] I go on duty every weekend but as nothing happens the earlier enthusiasm is slackening. Our hall is getting equipped splendidly now, great piles of blankets, wire stretchers and wooden stretchers, oilskin outfits, telephone and cars waiting their turn outside in case we get a sudden call. So different from the early days when we had to buy bandages from our own pockets and give threepence a week each to rent a room. The miners came to our aid with a penny weekly subscription each and from that the lovely hall was built. Of course the Government is supplying all this new equipment – it's wonderful what a war can do in a country which – two years ago – was sure to go bankrupt if they gave another ten millions to the old age pensioners. The wardens pay us a short visit every night, usually about the time we are making a cup of coffee and having some biscuits.[7] Their post is not yet so comfortable as ours.

~

It is a terrible job going to work during these nights of black velvet. The buses creep into the colliery area like great glow-worms carrying only the faintest light in front. After we leave the baths we have no light of any sort to guide us up the mountain incline. Sparks kicked up by our heavy boots are the only brightness we see. There must be near four hundred men on the night shift and they go out at about the same time, making a black army moving in the outside darkness, and start to tramp upwards along the narrow way to the colliery. A flooding river splashes far

---

[6] *The Thin Red Line* was a documentary radio programme dealing with military history.

[7] Air Raid Precautions (ARP) wardens.

below on our right and a line of whitened posts marks the danger edge of the ravine – but the coal dust from one day's working makes that white an almost invisible grey. The crowd of men stumble on through the darkness to something that is higher up – to me it seems a symbol of the times. They touch one another so that they shall have guidance. When one kicks an obstruction he warns the others, when someone falls down hands shoot out to help him swiftly to his feet – just as life should be, isn't it?

Every night we hear a trembling call when about half way up: 'Mind me, boys, I'm in by here!' We know it is an oldish man who is walking down in front of the rest of the afternoon shift. It is the cry of the aged, bewildered by happenings and fearing the advancing men – just as we fear the events of our time. As the crowd passes his refuge he adds his conclusions: 'Awful times these is boys; Like bats in the dark; that's what we are. There's a mess they have made of our world, haven't they.' And the chorus comes back 'By God! You're right. They have made a mess.' Later we meet the afternoon shift; that narrow roadway is packed as a thousand men struggle to pass one another. We get bitter against the other shift because of the conditions under which we have to meet them. They bump into us and we return the knocks with interest, they swear at us and we return the language, until we get to almost hate one another – all because of the conditions under which we struggle and the need for a little light – and understanding. So like our world.

~

It seems that our democracy has a lot to learn. Whilst most of the men are decent and a proportion are really cultured there is a section – possibly a quarter – who behave like animals. Anything left loose in the baths is stolen, even to working boots and brass fittings. Soap is taken if left in the open for a short while and coats disappear forever if left outside the lockers. One trouble is that the lockers are not big enough to take all the clothes. Sometimes we catch the thief and often he is a man who has no need to steal, then he is punished. But at other times we are up against a problem such as when a sixteen-year-old boy was caught wearing a man's boots. There were no soles to his own and he was putting the borrowed ones back at the end of his shift. He was the only one working in his home and had a crippled father. Seven shillings a week was going out of his small wages for bus fares. They did not have enough money to buy food and a new pair of working boots was an impossibility. What could we do? If we got the boy sacked or imposed a fine we would be penalising poverty still more. We have had cases of men who have passed the lavatories and used the cubicles at the baths as lavatories – there is no leniency for men of that type when they are caught. The men's interests at the baths are watched by a sub-committee who report to the general committee of which I am a member. I smashed three fingers of my left hand yesterday, but am trying to nurse them along and carry on. The maximum compensation is thirty shillings a week and the first three days are cropped, so I would not be entitled to more than fifteen shillings for the first week. If I can endure for two days my wages will equal that amount.

~

So far the most obvious sign of the war is that we are working full-time and that lost days from work do not trouble us any more. Food is not so plentiful, surely, but then we never had much choice in comparison to the big towns. My wife was always amazed and delighted by the choice of eatables when she visited Swansea (thirteen miles away) or Neath (seven miles). Neath is a clean and attractive town, reminding me in many ways of my native Hereford. Wattie felt the need for a little variety in his food whilst we were eating ours at about three o'clock last Wednesday morning. During his hunting about he found where a man had hidden a jar of pickles so that he could use them when he ate his food. That collier was in bed sleeping, so Wattie helped himself to a couple of onions. Crush Williams, another of my mates was with us at that meal. He suggested,

'A pint or two along of that would be OK, Wattie.'

'It would that,' Wattie agreed, 'and he's a queer bloke, he brings stone ginger to work 'cos there's some empty bottles in his stall. Shall I pop and see if there's one as is hid?'

'Go to hell,' Crush was disgusted, 'what d'you think I am. Stone ginger! By God!'

We go to work in pitch darkness and it is still dark when we come out. Daylight is creeping slowly over the mountains by the time we have bathed and are ready for home. In the old days before the baths every man was dozy and nodding in his seat whilst we waited for the late-comers, now they stay in the canteen until all are ready and are quite perky on the way home. On Saturday morning they are especially jubilant, with the knowledge of a week's work done and themselves going home clean to their families. Each has a leather bag – supplied by the baths – in which we take our singlets, shirts and pants home for washing on the weekend. We look, and act, like a gang of men going to market.

~

I think the monotony of the war is making us all slack and indifferent. So little has happened as we expected – in fact very little seems to have happened at all. Crush was in Gallipoli during the last war and he is contemptuous of present conditions. 'Call this a war,' he protests, 'when all they are doing is stand in their trenches and make faces at one another.' We are confident that the Maginot Line cannot be forced, or that it will cost a million lives to do so, and that in a waiting war we must win. Anyway it is giving our side ample time to add to even those strong defences they have in France.

Whilst we were waiting for our bus to be filled last Thursday morning I watched a man trying to carry some small wooden sleepers from one side of the colliery screens to the other. It would have been reasonable work for a healthy man but this one had to progress by slow and laboured steps. When the short journey was over he had to lean for a while against the railings whilst the strain of his breathing lifted his shoulders and convulsed the upper part of his body.

Each loaded step was a fierce effort; each journey was a torture that might mean collapse on the way. We watched him, dreading the sight but unable to help. We had all known him. He was a collier disabled by silicosis and because he was liked by some of the higher officials he was given the privilege of doing this 'light employment' for the last few weeks in which he could struggle to work. In those faltering steps and heaving gasps we could foresee our future.

~

How difficult it seems for some to adapt themselves to new ideas. I regard pit-head baths as one of the finest things to come into our lives, yet something like ten per cent of the men will not use them, although all have to pay the sevenpence a week for maintenance. I can see no excuse for this attitude unless the man has some complaint he seeks to hide – or a skin disease. I got on a service bus last Friday and passing one colliery eight miners got on. Three had bathed and out of the other five who had not four were officials – just the men who claim to set an example. I puzzled over the reason and could only conclude that when they had washed there was nothing to distinguish them from the ordinary miner; but their hats, rounded sticks, and general working attire showed them to be officials – so they wore that dress as long as possible. They should have been compelled to walk because they soiled the clothes of other passengers and left coal dust on the seats for those who followed. I remember when our baths were opened some of the firemen wanted to be put by themselves to wash apart from the miners but the management squashed that idea very promptly. Officials and men pay the same weekly contributions. Crush put forward an argument about the baths that had not occurred to me. He said that no doubt pit-head baths had saved scores of children from being scalded to death. The idea is good too, for the buckets and baths of hot water were dangerous to the children.

We seem to be plastered with new problems at our colliery and it seems every advantage of the times is being taken. Customs are broken and wage-rates reduced so often that we have to meet two and three nights a week. Now that strikes are not allowed we have hardly any power and the management take full advantage of it. War seems, to them, an opportunity for robbing our men in every way under the excuse of patriotism. One official told me that when Hitler won there would be an end to this humbugging with the Federation. I answered that if Hitler did win there might be many things on the company's side that might be altered too.

~

As we were leaving the mouth of the drift last Tuesday we heard a terrific roar high overhead. It seemed not many yards above us but we could not see far in the dim light. It passed by and eased into the distance then suddenly returned and seemed rushing just above where we stood half-way up the mountain side. We noticed a light moving up in the grey cloud and realised it was an aeroplane. We get them over every day but this roar was unusual, besides it had not yet got to daylight. Somebody called 'There's a parachute' and sure enough we could see one dropping, then another and finally five altogether dropping down lazily towards the valley. We watched them all land in far different areas. Then there was a rush to find if they were Germans. None of them were hurt much and it was an English bomber. The plane crashed into the mountain side about fifty yards from Wattie's bungalow. It was a show-place for days and hundreds walked up there. I had quite a piece of aluminium as a souvenir. Wattie says that is the only morning his wife has been up with breakfast ready for him.

~

It was a grey Christmas Eve with the firs looking chilled on the mountain side. We went around looking for an old log to saw up so that the real Christmas fire should crackle in our grates. Boys wheeled small sacks of coal picked from the tips and carried bunches of holly homewards to the villages. We had a holly tree at the end of the garden. The robins came to tap at the window as if asking for a bit of that Christmas dinner on account. The last of the acorns are falling like a shower of hail. We got a tiny fir tree from the plantation and hung it with some small presents. As dusk came the forestry workers went clumping home and a timber lorry stopped to give them a lift on top of the load. Away they went singing 'Good King Wenceslaus'. And as I passed the New Inn later that night it sounded that the 'Christians were awakening' in a real good humour. I slept with our two boy visitors and from about half past three they woke me continually with the question 'Have he come yet?' At daylight I told them to go downstairs and see – thinking to get some sleep after they had discovered their presents. Instead they dragged them back up for my inspection so I finally got up about nine o'clock.

~

I stood on the roadside watching the last few minutes of 1939 passing. It used to be the habit to signal the New Year in with all the colliery hooters in the valley blowing but that is not done during wartime. Almost at midnight a huge lumbering lorry passed me; its rattle showing it must have been laden with tin. Tight behind, with its horn clamouring for passage rushed a small car. The lorry kept to the middle until both passed from my sight. I saw it as the sign of an old broken year being rushed away by the new. Looking back on the war period of 1939 we feel that it has been a war of our minds more than bodies. We here have been almost untouched but our minds have been attacked by our enemies and soothed by our own side. They are afraid to attack, so we are told, and we are so well-prepared that it would be suicide. Our defences in France are too strong and the Army there growing every week. It seems it must go on like this for years and we are always told that time is on our side. I am told by almost everyone that the war is already over and that Hitler will give in before the summer. It seems too good to be true.

~

I have always been interested in the Russian situation. I felt that they were attempting a lead to the whole world in their new method of government. I realised how far behind they were at the beginning and how much they had caught up. Also that in many ways they were in front of us in this country. I was disgusted when Chamberlain abandoned them in favour of Germany at Munich, and there is not the least doubt in my mind that Chamberlain and many more of our leaders helped and encouraged Hitler to rearm in the hopes that he would do what they had failed to accomplish – crush Russia. The Russo-German pact was a surprise to me, but after consideration I decided we deserved it: yet it did open the way for Hitler to go to war. Then the Russian advance into Poland was a shock and the action disgusted me, until I saw that the Polish leaders had abandoned the battle and that the Germans would have taken that ground if Russia had hesitated. I have not heard of any Russian atrocities in that area – even the Conservative papers seem unable to discover any as yet.[8] And it seemed significant that the only time the Nazis have given back ground to

[8] In fact the Red Army murdered over four thousand Polish officers in the Katyn Forest near Smolensk in March 1940.

another army is in this Polish advance when they moved back before the Russians. But the Russian attack on Finland has knocked out all my ideals.[9] I can see it as nothing less than a brutal aggression. I cannot believe that Finland intended attacking Russia and am sure that our country will not want more war for a while after Germany is finished. Whatever Russia will gain in Finland must be balanced against the loss of sympathy throughout the world. I think it was a bad move. At the same time I am very glad that we did not do what Hore-Belisha screamed for us to do – go to war with Russia.[10] I do not believe these tales of the impotence of the Russian Army nor those of hundreds of thousands killed every day for the loss of about three Finns.[11] Edward Ward seems amateurish in his reporting for the BBC.[12] He is so obviously biased and incapable of drawing a fair conclusion, also his manner is so poor. Lord Haw-Haw is yards superior to him as a microphone personality.[13] He does get it over, although we know it is only a splash of truth in a pool of lies. The feebleness of our own programmes is driving us to explore the air further.

~

Bitter weather this January and the workmen's buses are hours on the road. Some of the afternoon shift are not home until four in the morning then the drivers have to start straight back with the day-men. There is a very bad way from Merthyr here – about sixteen miles – and there are so many ups and downs that the buses are often unable to get here at all and the men have to walk back for some miles without getting to work at all whilst their mates are waiting at the other end for the bus that never comes. This is one great advantage of the baths: the men are clean and

[9] Russia attacked Finland on 30 November 1939.
[10] Leslie Hore-Belisha, Minister of War, 28 May 1937–16 January 1940.
[11] By the end of 1939 the Russians had lost approximately 27,500 dead against a total figure of 2,700 Finnish dead and wounded.
[12] Edward Ward was a BBC War Correspondent, subsequently captured by the Italians in the Western Desert.
[13] Lord Haw-Haw was the popular nickname given to William Joyce, an Irish-born former member of the British Union of Fascists, who broadcast wartime propaganda on behalf of Nazi Germany.

have a warm canteen to wait in and they are respectable enough to travel by train if one is available, although the extra fare takes a dose out of their wages. I notice the bus drivers use the canteen well also, and some have frequent baths.

~

The Federation Secretary was waiting for me when our bus unloaded us by the baths last Wednesday night. A message had just come through about a Conference in Cardiff and I was to be the delegate. It was a bitter night with the wind lashing the sleet against us. As I was equipped with food ready for work I decided to work the shift and go to Cardiff early next morning. I got a grudging permission to come out a little early, washed about half-past five and tramped nearly three miles home through the tempest.

I caught a Red and White bus that passes the door after I had shaved and perked up a bit. About half-past eight we were on the way. Things were bad in our valley but when we had grunted up the three miles of slope and neared Hirwain we began to think we had dropped into the Arctic Circle. The roads were deep in snow, and scarcely one telegraph pole was unbroken. I kept warm by stumbling out of the bus to help the driver and conductor shift broken poles and wires out of the way. Cars were stranded all along the road but we ploughed slowly on through an Aberdare that had no semblance to the 'sweet 'Berdar' that I have always thought was an exaggeration. We smoozed on past Mountain Ash and Abercynon and through a slimy and grimy Pontypridd. Some of the dips and turns on this road are breathtaking on ordinary days but on this occasion it was marvellous that we got along at all. There are streets and roads where the bus seems to stand on end, and turns where it seems that only elastic vehicles could round. What it must be after dark in the blackout takes some imagining. Another wonderful thing to me is that human families can live in some of these surroundings and still keep sane. It is almost unbelievable that they should have a feeling for decency and a love of beauty after passing many years there. It was nearly half-past eleven before I reached Cardiff but my lateness did not matter because everyone else was late. Two more delegates got on the bus after Pontypridd – I could tell their trade and business by their appearance – and I got talking to them, then they guided me to the Cory Hall.

You hand your delegate's card in near the door and get a slip to sign. I was representing a thousand men. I was paid my day's wages, exact bus fare, and a small allowance for food. The Conference was to consider a formula for adjusting the wages to the cost of living. I was not very perky and had some difficulty in following some of the speeches which dealt with decimal points and other minute matters. No time is wasted at these Conferences. Arthur Horner sees to that and the South Wales Miners' Executive were seated behind him in the choir seats – I never saw such an unlikely looking lot of choir boys in my life.[14] The Cory Hall is a very bad place for sound and I was sleepy, hungry, and cold, so was mighty glad when the Conference ended. Could not get near the snack counter at Woolworths so wandered around and by luck stumbled into a small place – Italian I think – where I got a pot of tea and two steak and kidney pies warm. That revived me a little and I ambled back to the bus station.

It was still a dreary day and I welcomed every mile that took me nearer home. I could feel my whole body chilling up as we journeyed back through that long journey but the most terrible sight I have ever seen in housing was brought back to me when I looked through the frosted window as the bus began to drop down the long slope back into our valley. High up on the hillside a row of wooden army huts was placed just after the last war – they were second-hand huts when built. Miners and their families have been living in them ever since, although any up-to-date farmer would hesitate about putting chickens in them. They could get no repairs done and for a time withheld their rent but a magistrate's orders made them pay. They were paying about twelve shillings a week. Under those terrible conditions they lived – fronting the main road with the wind blowing under the sheds. I knew the men who lived in them and three gave their lives in work to retain that sort of shelter over their families. Once we took a man home there, badly injured. His wife was in bed with pneumonia and the water was dropping on her pillow.

[14] Arthur Horner, President of the South Wales Miners' Federation, 1936–46.

Finally in a journey that seemed endless we peered through the windows and judged we were near our home. I struggled out and stamped my feet and beat my hands. We were near in our guess and I stumbled in near the fire like a lost Arctic explorer. It took me a very long while to ease my shivering and all I could do was lie down for the rest of the evening. Am positive that I would not have survived many more hours on the road under those conditions. Of course I had been more than twenty-four hours without sleep and had worked hard in a warm atmosphere the night before. I did not work the following night and for some reason did not even catch cold. My iron constitution I expect – or what my wife calls my iron nature.

~

I gave the report of that Conference this week, Friday night. I took a deal of care and enlarged from my notes until I had about two thousand words. Last Sunday night I went out and tried it on the trees and as they seemed to take it in good part I left it at that. I knew there would be two or three hundred waiting to hear my report and as the weather was still bitter cold I arrived early and decided that one glass of Guinness would give me the necessary boldness and eloquence. Half-way through that drink the Chairman crept in, apparently having decided in like manner. I accepted a second dubiously and we left afterwards. After the minutes came my turn. I hopped on the platform, slackened my coat, placed the notes on the table impressively and rattled off the report in a manner worthy of Winston Churchill. Everyone gave me high praise, except the Secretary, who objects to any report that is not given by himself – and my report would have lasted him for three hours. It took another Guinness to ease the dryness in my throat afterwards. My mates underground suspect that I am on a 'snip' when I go in my turn to these conferences. In fine weather it might not be so bad but as I total up the hours since I started to walk home, then all the time going to Cardiff, and back as well as the Conference, the time in writing out my report and journeying to the colliery meeting to deliver it I am quite sure the easier way would have been to have worked my regular shift at the mine.

~

We have found a method of making the journey to work easier. Now we wrap old newspapers around our bodies and that shows the other shift where we are. Some of them were quite alarmed at the first appearance; they seemed to think it was a ghost coming. Now they call out 'What's the news to-night, butty?' The villages are gloomy shells after dark with only faint signs to show they are open. The children no longer play their games in the light of the shop windows. They are taking great interest in ARP matters here now and training hard. I had my first certificate in it some months ago and my thirteenth for ambulance work. A real ARP rehearsal was quite a flop last week for owing to a confusion of telephone messages our ambulance went in the wrong direction and the relief ambulance broke down and was over an hour late. I thought the lady driver was quite a sedate miss until she gave me her account of the arrival at the wrong place – she was a good swearer, by Golly. Crush would have been proud to welcome her as a mate.

~

Had another full dress rehearsal this week in which an old stable was supposed to be bombed. The Fire Brigade dropped on the fire like lightning and squashed it definitely and at once – much to the regret, apparently, of the crowd who were there and felt the fire had not been given a sporting chance. I go on duty every Saturday night but it is more or less a matter of form as we doze or sleep or talk the time away.

~

We had a visitor this Sunday afternoon. He was neatly dressed in blue and well-brushed as to boots and hair. He gave me a religious tract with the manner of a man who hands over a great gift and then informed the garden and the valley generally that 'God is good', which statement was repeated by the badge in his button-hole. I will give him this credit – that as far as I have ever known Jim has tried to live up to his religion and has never sworn or drunk, nor has he robbed his fellow workers. When he was himself robbed he protested firmly but in moderate language and his retort to an overman who had blatantly cheated him is still spoken of with awe in our colliery. He said 'What you have done to me is downright robbery. Downright robbery, I repeat, but I feel that God will punish you. Good morning.' Just like that. The fact that he did not use one swear word and actually wished the official good morning caused a sensation amongst the men – and astounded the overman.

Jim has worked well for the company during more than thirty years, now he is disabled by silicosis. It is an effort for him to walk, yet the light employment they offered him would have needed quick movement and an occasional run. Also it was in an exposed position on the mountain side and Jim's breathing would not survive one cold morning. When he failed to do it they knocked him off the books and all the help he could get was one and eightpence a week as he had partly paid for his house and he was ordered to mortgage and use that money before he could have help from the relieving officer – thus do we encourage thrift. We had been fighting his case and I was glad to tell him that we had managed to get an increase as partial compensation of a guinea a week. Now we are fighting for full compensation of thirty shillings or a job he can manage to do. 'The Lord has heard my call', Jim boomed, 'he will always provide.' Which was not much credit to us for our efforts as a committee.

~

Good many evacuees around here now. The sleeping quarters here are too small or else we would welcome a couple. Most of the local people go to a great deal of effort to make them comfortable and I know one old Welsh lady – a widow living in a large house – who has two young boys with her. She is childless and is tremendously anxious to make her young visitors happy. Her English is very poor and the evacuees are difficult to understand when they speak because their English is poor too, but from a different standpoint to the old lady's. She wraps them up and shelters them inside her home – which is full of lovely furniture. I think they have been brought up roughly and they seem frightened of this gentle and fragile old lady. I know they are complaining about being there – they are too sheltered. The old lady will be very grieved if she loses the boys and her very anxiety to please them is frightening her charges away. Sometimes it is very pathetic when there is need to part brothers and sisters on arrival. When I move about the valley

I see miners' wives taking little evacuee children for walks and explaining what goes on in the collieries to them. This war may do some good in that different people will learn how we live and that our country is not all coal tips or wild people. Here the valley is wide and very lovely and the mountains that border it are grand.

~

Wife very worried about the food problem as she has to make journeys to the shop every day to watch her share when it does come in; it means a two-mile journey each way. Often if she leaves it a day she finds her share of something has been given to another customer. She is savagely annoyed at the pictures of Cabinet Ministers and others having luncheons – and at the menus. One little meal we always enjoy is on the rare occasions when we go to Neath. There, in the markets, are several stalls where faggots and peas are sold for eating on the premises. We sit on benches and the room is cramped. While you eat you look out on the market and the passers-by look in at you. Home-made tart and cups of tea are sold also and the women proprietors know all the gossip about their customers and their friends or enemies. My wife would not dream of coming from Neath without her visiting her special faggot and pea stall. Very surely she is not alone in that liking for there is a long row of people always waiting for a vacant place at a table.

~

Had an idea that decoy lights could be placed on the waste land that stretches for miles across the top of these mountains. I thought enemy planes could be deceived and encouraged to drop their bombs by a system of partially-hidden lights over uninhabited land. Sent it to Home Secretary and had two very courteous and grateful replies – shall send other ideas if they happen along.

~

One mate is very bitter against a certain section of evacuees. It appears they are high school girls and have been sent to his area. He had one, she was somewhere about sixteen, rather a naughty miss, and they did all they could to oblige her. One night she asked, could she have the parlour for a night to entertain a boy friend. These people value their parlour highly: it is a sort of sacred room. I am against that attitude for I have memories of a mouldy room at home which was scarcely used except on the once yearly occasion when the vicar came to see us and collect the one-and-sixpence for the parish magazine. Anyway these people agreed to the request and lit a fire to assist the entertaining. Just before the visitor was due to arrive the housewife shyly explained that she was glad their visitor had got to know someone who would help to cheer her in this fresh place – was it a Welsh boy? 'No,' was the decided reply, 'it is not. For all it matters to you it might be a Chinese boy, or a black one, but it will certainly never be a Welsh one, they are too common.' The housewife became annoyed over that and pointed out that she should not have spoken in that manner to people who were doing their best under difficult conditions and wanted to make them comfortable. 'It is your duty,' the English miss informed her, 'and we have no desire to be here. It is simply unfortunate circumstances that have forced us to come.' Thus do the educated ones of our nation endear themselves to those they count as foreigners even in their own country. I was told of another from the same school who arrived at a miner's home and exclaimed 'Good gracious! No study for me! How on earth do you think I can manage without a study?' I am English born and have watched the evacuee children as they went homeward with the native children. I am bound to say that in speech, physique and manners the English children have no cause to claim superiority and in culture they are far behind the Welsh children who correspond to them in class.

Found a mate named Ernest walking along in the dark when I was coming out Wednesday morning, so I showed light to him and we went together. Half-way back is a place where the journey rope swings across and smacks against the side when it is working. I warned Ernest of this danger, then took so much care to show him light that I was late in getting across myself and the swinging rope caught me and banged me against the side. As I lay there the rope kept moving and sawing away at my ankles with the weight of ten trams of coal on it. I called twice to Erny asking him to grab the two signal wires and draw them together, thus causing the warning bell to ring in the engine-house but Erny stood stupidly by, making no move whilst the rope sawed away at my ankles and I was in agony. Finally I forced myself up, then grabbed the wires myself. The rope stopped and I twisted my legs from under it. 'Well I'm buggered!' was the limit of Erny's comment and action, but I was definite in my opinion of a man who did not have enough sense to stop the rope. I felt cold all over, then very hot; afterwards I felt weak inside, then became sick. My left leg was very painful and I had a short rest before starting the two-mile journey to the drift mouth. It is still very painful and feels that some time will pass before it is better.

~

The bump on the ankle of a week ago is still painful and the leg gives under me when I walk. It is all blue and have had a job to keep at work. It was a help, in a way, last Wednesday when my mate and myself were at work repairing a big hole from which a lot of stone had fallen. We had placed rings in position and then had to put nine-feet-long posts across from ring to ring and build timber above them until the upper stones were held firmly. These upper stones, about twenty feet high, were not looking solid but there was no way of securing them until we had the cross-timber. We had arranged sleepers on full trams as a staging and had got two posts in position; but when trying to lift the middle, and heavier, one my leg kept giving and at last we failed to get it up. I wanted to try again but my mate insisted on getting another man to help. Whilst he went after him I got down and went back for a drink. I heard a crash; and when I returned found that two large stones had fallen, smashing our staging. They had dropped without warning right on the spot where we had been trying to lift the post, and but for his insistence we might still have been struggling there when the stones dropped. Surely two tons at least.

~

March seems to get windier as it gets near the end. The sycamores are bending almost flat and the wind is rushing high above this house like an express train. The trees in the forestry plantation are waving like a great fan.

Last Monday I took a deal of time writing a letter to the

Minister of Mines. I made many suggestions which I am sure would be useful as I know the industry so well and have studied its problems. I suggested two of the men and two officials to see that all waste steel was sent outside and away – there is a vast amount wasted. I suggested that broken timber be sent out to the saw-mills and there sawn into foot-long lids or wedges to tighten posts – this would save new timber and would greatly lessen the danger of accidents. I suggested that coal dust should be loaded into small sacks and used instead of sandbags for fortifying the mining areas, and that all small bits of steel fishplates and damaged steel arches – a great many of these are seen every day underground – should be saved and used for shrapnel – also that they should study the structure of the ironstone that is found in some seams and is almost as hard as iron, to see if it could be used with shrapnel. I sent a pile of suggestions, and I know some were good: Oh yes, also the idea for spreading a film of coal dust to hide the glint of a flowing river by night – when raiders are likely.

Yesterday I had a letter that had been handed over ice: my suggestions had been noted. Thank you, Mr Minister, I will save time and stamps in future.

~

April with us and the garden coming really alive. A treat to walk around it now and discover fresh green shoots where only bareness was showing a few days ago. Queer how the hedges come into colour – not long ago they were grey-brown and seemingly dead, then a few little pecks of green showed. That green got larger and brighter until the spots seemed to dominate the brown background, then one day I looked at the hedge and it was turning green all over. Reminds me that I shall soon have to start the monthly trimmings which are needed to keep it in shape.

~

After all the bluster and the boasting about the way we were waiting to be attacked it seems that we have again been beaten on the jump – into Norway.[15] What on earth is the matter? Why are

[15] Germany invaded Norway on 9 April 1940.

we always caught on the wrong foot when we are supposed to be so perfectly prepared? Feeling is pretty angry in these parts against the Government.

On my own theory I would do a quick move now into Spain. I feel we would then rally the supporters of the defeated Government and would forestall Hitler or Mussolini. We would have such a vast coastline ready for bases then waiting for the day that I feel will surely come when they tire of twisting Chamberlain around their fingers and the ice-cream man believes it is time to do a bit of fighting or grabbing on his own.[16] At the Conference we were told that the reason South Wales miners could not expect a higher rise was because their coal mostly went to Italy and was sold there at almost cost price so that they should be kept neutral. In my opinion they are passing it on at a good profit to Adolf. We are now having a small rise of fivepence a day – not half-enough to counter the rise in food.

We are assured that the invasion of Norway is a bad tactical blunder and Churchill was devastating in his speech. I wonder, do the BBC realise what effect the broadcasting of some of those luncheon speeches has on people who have not enough food. There is a well-fed complacency about them that is maddening. The glasses tingle, superior voices bray their appreciation, and very often the voice of the speaker is thickened with wine and spirits. Wattie says that he could smell whisky over the wireless!

~

General feeling this week that the war is going to get a move on. More men are being taken from the mines. They are digging trenches in what we term a park. Why they do not re-open some of the old levels near the villages completely puzzles me. We have great natural advantages for shelters as the mountains run up steeply and men are available who could put the levels in safe order. They should be ideal for the purpose as they were worked with naked lights and the roof is so good that it is still unbroken after many years' neglect. People would be safe in there for weeks and they could be ready in a month. I think they would have been wiser to build a new factory that is being constructed here in the

---

[16] The 'ice-cream man' is probably a reference to Mussolini.

mountain. I feel the factories and the towns of the future will be built underground and here we have the right places, definitely. You can ventilate a pit so why not a factory – on a more elaborate scale? Am positive this new works could have been built inside the mountain with the smoke stacks horizontal and it would not have been much longer in the building because they are certainly very slow over it. News from Norway confusing; some suggestion that our troops were not equipped and trained in a manner suitable for the climate. That must be ridiculous because we were told they had 100,000 perfectly trained and equipped troops ready to send to Finland. We should look well now if Hore-Belisha's advice to declare war on Russia had been adopted. Seem to have quite enough as it is on our plate.

~

Apparently Hitler cannot stop the birds singing or the buds bursting for the garden is alive with sound. We almost feel that we regret the passing of winter as the long days will give a better chance for air-raids. Our planes are over continuously, on practice flights I suppose. We watch them as they pass just over the trees and seem sure to knock into the mountain. The primroses are showing and the daffodils in the idle church nearby are coming out a deep, rich, green. No doubt now that we have been left in the cart over Norway. Deep resentment against Chamberlain and Halifax in this area.[17] How can we expect to win a war with palsied old men who will not learn? The men who cheered Chamberlain after Munich seem the loudest in their complaints: 'Something badly wrong, obviously. Do they *want* to win?' Obvious that some change will have to be made. We have been bluffed all along.

~

This year the month was in before I saw the lovely blossom that bears the name of May. How attractive both the month and the blossom is. They seem to merge into our life without any bluster

[17] Viscount Halifax, Secretary of State for Foreign Affairs, 1 March 1938–23 December 1940.

and commotion. The days are fragrant with the perfume from the hedges and the smell of soil that is sending out growth. The rhododendrons are showy but their opening buds appear clumsy, the may flower just comes like scented snow that falls in the night. The walks around here are a sheer delight in these days of early summer for even the bracken shoots help with their pale greenness.

~

Somehow the rumours come into the workings during the night shifts. Usually we are dubious because some of the men outside have queer ideas about jokes and we often have to reverse the tales they send in – or wait until they are confirmed. Our bus driver is more staid and reliable; from him we get the early news and an account of what the night has brought in other areas. It was our driver who told us that Hitler had invaded Belgium.[18] Surely this was madness in his tactics. We would go to the help of Belgium at once. Later we heard that Chamberlain had resigned and that Churchill was forming a new government. Felt a sense of relief over this because I would rather fight a war with Churchill than endure a stalemate under Chamberlain. Regret that the shadow with the umbrella is still to be retained as a symbol of the Tory authority – better if he had retired, taking all his supporters with him.[19] Wonder if it is wise for Morrison, Bevin, and Greenwood to take office under the present circumstances.[20] If Toryism has failed why not compel them all to get out and have a real people's government – not a patch of one? However, we do feel more cheerful and prepared to work hard under the new direction. Little use to deny that there was scant enthusiasm for the way

[18] Germany invaded the Low Countries on 10 May 1940. Neville Chamberlain resigned and was replaced as Prime Minister by Winston Churchill on the same day, Churchill immediately forming a Coalition Government.

[19] The 'shadow with the umbrella' is a reference to Chamberlain, who remained in government as Lord President of the Council, despite stepping down as Prime Minister.

[20] These were all Labour politicians. Herbert Morrison became Minister of Supply, Ernest Bevin Minister of Labour, and Arthur Greenwood Minister without Portfolio.

things were going before – even the few that supported Neville were not convincing in their pleas. Our troops are being rushed into Belgium. Things are moving so swiftly that one can hardly keep record of them. We were told that Holland would be the watery grave of a million Germans. That seems one more fairy tale.[21]

~

Enemy planes flew continually along the valley right through last night. Never before have they kept so low and remained so long. When I got home, found the wife sleepy and worried. Peter and the wife had dressed, and hurried up to a clearing in the woods about one o'clock in the morning. There they spent some hours of misery, confident that they were to be bombed. If they hit this isolated house, so I assure her, it will be by accident because it is well concealed by high trees. Peter went back indoors to fetch a chair and blanket for his mother. I argued that there was less protection in the woods than indoors because the house is very strongly built. Think she fears suffocation chiefly, but it will be the house for me if they come close. There I shall stay whether they come by land or air.

~

What is the matter in France? We are now told that they have no guns to stop the tanks. Twelve months ago we were told that German tanks were made of plywood and fell to pieces if a man hit them with his fist. Gamelin was paraded for us as a superman who could not possibly make the least mistake.[22] It seems the Germans went through the finest army in the world like a knife cutting into cheese. Our local experts assure me that it is just a trap. The Germans have got through, they admit, but wait until

---

[21] The Netherlands surrendered on 15 May 1940.

[22] General Maurice Gamelin, the Supreme Commander of French forces, who also had overall command of the British Expeditionary Force.

they want to get back. Hope every day to hear that the gap is closed and part of the German Army cut off.[23]

~

Germans reaching the Channel ports this week and it seems we are impotent to stop them.[24] Will they come straight across? It is a thought that chills you when you realise that they will soon be in sight of our shores. Talk about chickens coming home to roost; how some of our leaders must wish they had supported Czecho-slovakia and accepted the help of Russia. Did the behaviour of French leaders then have something to do with the weakness of France's fighting now? Or are the French people not united at this time because of the let-down in those days? That is my only requiem for Chamberlain – he did his best to avoid war and helped the war-makers by so doing. Even we who believed in Pacificism and disarming in the past must admit it was a mistaken policy whilst the German mentality went armed – and whilst bitter grievances were left unsoothed in Europe.

~

Again it was our bus driver who staggered us with the news of the surrender by the Belgian King.[25] To us this seems a dastardly move. It is a betrayal and sacrifice of allies who have rushed to help him in the past and are at his side now. We are told he gave our leaders not the least warning.[26] History will have a different record of him compared to his father – history will have many things to say that are not flattering to the traditions of birth and breeding always showing up in a crisis. That is a yarn I have never believed and find contradicted every day. Training and heritage help to form a man but there is something that can be lacking when all advantages are given – and there is something that shows

---

[23] By 14 May the Germans had broken through the French front at Sedan.

[24] The Germans were close to the Channel ports by 26 May.

[25] Belgium surrendered on 28 May 1940.

[26] In actual fact Belgium had informed the French and British Military Missions before discussing surrender terms with Germany.

up when no good influence from birth or privilege can be traced. It is the inner nature of a man that counts and when we are advanced enough to give every man and child an equal chance we will find that out. These must be most anxious days for millions of our people. Churchill hinted at very bad news. I expect he meant about our men who are deserted in Belgium. It shows the weight of the German war machine that such an army as we have there is quite unable to check their advance. Something must happen, please God some of our men will be saved. Wonder if it will be possible for them to cut their way through. It is a relief to feel that we have a fighter in charge; what the state of things in this country would be now if the Government had not been changed is not cheerful thinking. Reports that our men are fighting grandly and that some have been taken off.

~

A lovely June, when our land is indeed smiling. Our usual observation is 'If everything was only as good as the weather.' It seems almost unbelievable that so many of our troops should have been rescued from Dunkirk but our hearts beat again now we have them safe.[27] I saw two of them who were home for a couple of days. Their nerve seemed badly-shaken but both stated they wanted to go on with the fight so that we could get rid of 'the sods that are in Germany and in this country'. Apparently war has made them real democrats. There can be little doubt that authority has blundered badly once again. I thought we were superbly equipped and ready for anything. They tell a different tale – so do the LDV when we get talking.[28] Where have the millions been going? Some one has let us down again and the flesh and blood of the workers had to stem the breach. The idea of a class that was born to rule seems to have crashed completely for never could men have been more incapable.

[27] The evacuation of Dunkirk, involving the rescue of over three hundred thousand Allied troops, took place between 26 May and 4 June.
[28] Local Defence Volunteers or 'Home Guard'.

Italy has at last come into the open.[29] Somehow it has not been much of a shock to us. Possibly Chamberlain may feel some surprise, but he was a man incapable of learning. At one conference, as I said, we were told that the reason South Wales miners could not have a rise in wages was because their coal had to be sold at a very low rate to Italy – so that they should stay neutral – and pass the coal on at a profit. We had a few Italians working with us and none of them had any enthusiasm for Mussolini – but they have not been in their native land since childhood and have reared families here. They seem good parents and citizens, but have been interned. Most of the cafés and ice-cream shops in Wales are run by Italians, somehow they do it better than Welshmen and certainly they get the trade. I feel that this declaration of war by Italy is just telling us what we have known for a long while and this open enemy is better than a false friend. It is tough going on France however and a coward's blow to them. No one, especially those who fought in the last war, has any respect for the fighting qualities of the Italians.

~

More details of Dunkirk, showing how wonderfully the little ships and men acted. Thank God we're not all born to rule and trained to think our every action must be right and above criticism. French seem completely disorganised and I feel they will lose most of France before they make a stand. The swallows in our porch have been unlucky this year. They were delighted when they found the nest in the porch, undisturbed. At once they started to at the work of rearing another family. Like many humans they judged that a little improving of the old home was needed – and in like manner they made a mess of it. They carried down and feathers to re-line the nest, but when the young were feathering the nest had been made too shallow and one by one they fell out. We tried to revive them and place them back but the nest was too difficult of approach. I wondered what the parent birds would do about it. They made no effort to deepen the nest, instead they started to build another and I watched their method. The weather

---

[29] Italy declared war on France on 10 June, and on Britain on 11 June.

had been rainless for many days and the clay which they carried would not stick. They abandoned the underside of the slates and picked a new place high up against a beam. They scratched this beam deeply with their beaks and in the grooves started to build the foundation of their new nest. It took them all of a week, working every minute of daylight and now apparently we shall have to be careful how we sit in the porch or we may have a present from above. Peter has written a card which he intends to place near the old nest if he can find a ladder. It reads 'This desirable residence to let, furnished.'

~

Pétain, whom we were told was to take over in France to repeat his 'They shall not pass' policy of the last war, is surrendering France.[30] What can have happened to this once great country that they so easily surrendered to their eternal enemy? I think it must be very great fear and distrust of one another amongst the people because if there had been any sort of fighting spirit this never would have happened. The best army in the world – something bad must have sapped their strength! Now we are alone and the storm will surely be on us soon. The weather seemed mockingly ideal as if to say look how sweet a land you are soon to lose. There does seem a different spirit amongst people for although we can be sure that Churchill is no friend of the working class he is at least a man with some fight and imagination in his nature. He is definitely the leader we want in war and the inclusion of Bevin and Morrison has soothed our conscience a little. I think Halifax should have been shifted and sometimes I feel the Labour men were wrong to take any office until the old gang were completely ousted. Somehow we have no liking or faith in Attlee, and yet have confidence in Archibald Sinclair, although he is a rich man and a Liberal.[31] We still have a soft spot for old Lloyd George, despite his acrobatics in the past.

[30] Marshal Pétain, the hero of the Battle of Verdun in 1916, on 16 June 1940 replaced Reynaud as Prime Minister of France, and immediately opened negotiations with Germany for a surrender. An armistice was concluded on 22 June.

[31] Clement Attlee, the leader of the Labour Party, became Lord Privy Seal in 1940. Archibald Sinclair, the leader of the Liberal Party, was not given office in the War Cabinet.

~

Things very quiet and we are recovering from recent shocks. Still feel that war effort is not affecting some people at all and see too many able men with nothing to do, and no intention of altering it. Enemy planes are passing now but they seem only concerned at planning the land. No military objective here but plenty less than ten miles away in both directions. Are assured that the mountains will protect us and some talk learnedly about air-pockets and cross winds. Hope that they are right and that bombs will have proper respect for air-pockets. They are building barriers along the roads hurriedly and the LDV are gaining in strength and skill. Strange how this idea caught on so swiftly; there are hundreds of them in every decent-sized village. Why is it that so many joined a thing that was concerned with shooting and so few are attracted to the ambulance service? Perhaps the idea of a difficult training may frighten some but what a benefit the training would prove all through life. One thing I would like to see is that there should be some way of working up from an ambulance man to a doctor. At present money bars the way and I have known men who have worked at ambulance duties for thirty years – born healers – and had very little thanks, no pay, and no possible chance of getting farther in the profession for which they were so obviously suited.

~

Still a breathing space, unexpected. Still nature mocks us with a lovely summer and the scent of the roses and lavender blows into and around our noses. It is difficult to assess the cause of France's disaster – I would have gambled they would have fought on to the last inch. I read that more than three-quarters of a million trained French soldiers never fired one shot for their country. If the truth is ever told it will surely be astounding. Not only countries are crumbling, traditions are crumbling too and the worship of class.

~

A mid-August in which Nature is kind but our hearts are fluttering. The moon is full in a clear sky and we know the tides are high. Will this be invasion night? That is what we have asked ourselves every night. What will be with us when we next come out into the daylight? Will they have landed and advanced – the sea is not more than eight miles away and high tide swells the river below this house. We are living in the swing of history; no need to dwell on the past glories for we are making records for the future every day. We study the weather each night as we go in to work and ask eagerly of the incoming morning shift or the bus drivers what is the latest news. They have been busy at the concrete barriers on the roads and the Home Guards stand watching continually. We stare at the mountain slopes and wonder if they will be kind to parachute troops and if men will have to die to defend them. But the critical day and night passes quietly, another period goes and a gale passes with it. We breathe freely again, it seems we are still secure. The weather is delightful and surely there never was a finer year for roses. They are massed on the fences and the honeysuckle brightens and perfumes the hedges. Above this house the ground slopes up to a quarry – probably the place where the stones that form this house were taken. The passing of centuries has soothed the roughness of the stones, now the gaps in the quarry are hidden by honeysuckle. When the wind blows from that angle it brings with it the scent of honeysuckle and we draw our breath in with an ecstatic 'ah-hah'. In the early morning we get the pine scents too – like inhaling medicine.

~

Convoys are passing along this road almost every day. Have counted over a hundred vehicles in one passing. Had a long procession of lorries driven by women drivers last Wednesday. After a long and detailed study I decided that either women don't look their best when in uniform or they have sent the really good-looking ones by another route. Planes over continually, never are sure whether they are ours or Germans and the warning system is still all shapes. Sometimes we get a warning after an enemy plane – judged by engine sound – has been over us for half-an-hour. Sometimes we get the 'all clear' whilst the guns are banging and the plane sounds right overhead.[32] Saturday afternoon the ice-

---

[32] There were frequent air-raids in the Swansea and Neath areas from the end of June to mid-October 1940.

cream man stopped his cart opposite our place whilst he served us with some wafers and a lot of gossip. A convoy came along and most of the lorries pulled up. From them hurried driver after driver wanting a threepenny wafer; after which they climbed back into place and drove away controlling the lorry with one hand and the ice-cream with the other. It seemed such a contradiction – the men of war as eager for a sup of ice-cream as were the children.

~

No August holidays this year as our coal is so badly needed. Yet the colliery officials are being given, and are taking, their fortnight's holiday with pay as usual. The working miner is not allowed to take his week, even if he wants to. We are thrilled by the exploits of our air fighters. They must be wonderful. The Air Force and our Navy are a grand shield and seem able to withstand the blunderings of our politicians. There is a sickening dread when we realise what is happening and what will happen to London because we feel it is such a big area that no bombs can miss if dropped in that vicinity. There can be little open land there to ease the damage and very surely it will be the women and children of the poor who will suffer most. The news makes us feel more brotherly to some of the visitors and not to take so seriously the affected superiority of some of the evacuees.

~

It seems that the song of the birds has slackened earlier than usual this year. Possibly the dread that is in the minds of all humans has spread to our feathered consolers; or it may be that the strange objects that drone above have alarmed the birds for it seems to be only the swallows that come swooping down from the sky. Aeroplanes are in our hearing night and day. The nights are dreaded by my wife and boy as there is the fear of invasion and I have to go to work. I assure her that this house has immense strength and that a bomb would have to land directly on it before the walls would weaken as they are a yard thick in stone. She fears the landing of parachute troops and there is some excuse because it is a long distance to the next dwelling. I suppose it is the thought of this danger that makes her want to move nearer other people. She is quite content on the Saturday nights when I am at home. Every working night we worry about what will have happened by the time we get home again and we feel some security at seeing the road barriers guarded by troops.

~

If this continual warning and raiding goes on we will be having a crop of nervous diseases after this war. What must be the feelings of invalids who cannot leave their beds? And of pregnant women? What sort of children will they bring into this frightened world? Three and four times a night they are alarmed by the warning hooters and the wardens seem quite as frightening for the choice of men seems very unsuitable in many cases. Loud-voiced, and excitable men are not the type I would choose for that job. As there are no shelters anywhere near here what do they gain by disturbing the people when there is no place in which they can hide? I feel it would be wiser to keep the warnings quiet and to let folks sleep if they can.

~

September fair in Neath was very quiet this year. Only the stock fair was held. I went down so that I could revive my early acquaintance with farming and somehow I feel I have a right to look at a cow and a horse even now. This sale was very leisurely and no one seemed concerned when the time for starting had passed by more than an hour. The horses were chiefly of the pit-pony stamp and good ones sold well – but they were few . . . As things went tame I wandered up the slope towards the Gnoll.[33] I knew a few bombs had been dropped up that way and thought I might see some damage. Everything was very quiet and I strolled along. I saw a rope lying flat on the road but the pavement was clear and eventually I stood where the pavement had been mended with tarred stones and some bricks were disturbed from a wall. Whilst I was considering this I saw a policeman waving from

---

[33] Gnoll House was an eighteenth-century mansion located in a large park, the home of Sir Humphrey Mackworth, one of the founders of the copper-smelting industry in Neath.

the other end. I walked slowly up to meet him. 'How did you get there?' he asked. 'Easy', I answered, 'just walked up from the fair ground.' 'Good God,' he was surprised, 'don't you know that lot is evacuated?' 'What for?' I inquired. 'Two unexploded bombs, big ones,' he answered, 'and you was lingering the other side of the wall from them.' 'Oh I see,' I replied, 'then I s'pose I'd better clear off this way.' And I did.

~

As I was waiting outside for the workman's bus last Thursday I heard a succession of crashes – quite close. The wife rushed out but I persuaded her – aided by a most sensible Peter – that she was mistaken and they were only gunfire from near Neath. At last she went back in. When the bus arrived they told me bombs had dropped not very far away and had shaken the bus badly. They had jumped out and taken shelter alongside the hedge. Next day we went to see the craters – not very far from this place. The first had dropped not many yards from the end of some houses and altogether nine had been dropped without hitting one house. He had laid a track of holes right across the mountain – starting near one village and finishing just before reaching the other. We are getting tales of near escapes from the men when they come from Merthyr and Aberdare, whilst the Port Talbot men are suffering from bombing almost every night. They are eager for details from the bus driver every morning and I frequently hear them speaking their anxiety as to how things are at home during the night.

~

Our Friday night committee meetings used to be disturbed by the coal journeys passing alongside the small cabin in which we meet and in which dues are paid. Nowadays – or nights – another sound disturbs us, the drone of enemy planes just above. It is a small cabin and very stuffy when every window and crevice must be tight closed to prevent a light showing. When we come from there the outside darkness blinds a man. I walk into walls and do all sorts of silly things along a road I know well. Most of the way there are no curbstones and one only locates oneself by falling over a piece of pavement and by falling realising that the bus junction is near. I was waiting at about nine o'clock last Friday night when a plane passed right above and dropped a line of incendiaries. Most of them fell on waste land and burnt themselves out, some fell near some bungalows and were soon extinguished. Next day they traced some unexploded bombs and set them off, giving a deal of alarm to the people who had not been warned and were undecided whether it was a colliery explosion or not.

~

The tea ration hits us badly because that is about the only drink we use regularly. I was very surprised to notice that most of my mates were very concerned over this new ration. I heard some of them arguing how many spoonsful of tea they would have to allot to themselves. The bachelors seem especially concerned. I expect the maiden ladies are too, but they do not come within my experience.

Strange how people's natures always assert themselves. The quiet ones endure the raids with serenity although they probably feel most deeply. The noisy ones are the upsetters under all conditions. I have heard women rushing about calling, 'They'll be dropping bombs on us all in a minute,' and another telling a child, 'You run away or you'll be blown to bits.' That was the typical mentality of the shouters.

~

They had been having nightly alarms at the ambulance hall but somehow Saturday night – my duty – had always been silent and peaceful, so much so that some had hinted that there must be some arrangement between the German airmen and myself. Last night I was again on duty, and they were resting after a busy week. We were quite sure that the usual arrangement would continue and although planes passed over us we were not so much concerned. It was a filthy night for July, rather cold and with rain sheeting the valley. Cars were standing in the dark outside our hall and the water was splashing over them. A special constable had come in to tell us the enemy planes were above – which we knew – and to drink a cup of our coffee. We could detect the rising and falling of the engine sound as the planes circled high overhead.

Just afterwards there came a thunderous roar which seemed to move the mountains. It stopped our breathing for some seconds – it was the first high explosive bombs we had heard. A few seconds later the hooters moaned their warning. We answered a call for help but it came from the next area and they were able to handle all the casualties – not so many.[34]

~

A quiet week except for Tuesday morning. Peter was in Neath and it was a lovely day with a clear sky and a bright sun. Everyone was going about their business as if no such horror as war existed. A plane came along in the distance, but no one seems to have taken much notice, probably they thought it was one of ours practising, and anyway Neath had no defences or military objectives. Suddenly that plane swooped out of the sky, dropped a series of bombs, used a machine-gun, then rose and flew away. He left death and destruction behind. I saw one of the houses later. It had taken a direct hit and not a dish or piece of furniture was usable again. A young woman, sister to a mate of mine, was in the kitchen and was knocked unconscious, but recovered and had only a few scratches as a result. The gas pipes were completely flattened, and a two-shilling piece on the mantelpiece was curled up like a dried leaf but on searching we found a cardboard box with six eggs inside and not one was cracked. What accounts for such fragile things as eggs surviving a blow that had knocked a house down?

~

Defence preparations are moving around here now. We can see barrage balloons glittering in the sky towards the sea. We have become used to the gruff barking of guns and my mates are talking of bombs falling and guns shelling in as normal a manner as they once discussed football. Wattie went out last Tuesday night and while down the garden he heard such a queer noise that he bolted into the house at top speed – to his wife for protection, I expect. It was a barrage balloon collapsing and it knocked part of

[34] Coombes's short story 'Sabbath Night', published in *Folios of New Writing* (Autumn 1940), gives an account of a similar episode.

the chimney off. Lightning struck it I suppose, but Wattie claims he was quicker than lightning getting inside. Mate complains bitterly about the attitude of the assessor who examined him concerning the air-raid damage. 'Once I hoped that it wouldn't happen to no other chap,' he told me; 'Now I hopes it will happen to him, and he be in the house.'

~

Mid-October, with a shiver coming in the wind. The nights are again long stretches of solid darkness and we have to grope for our every step outside the house whilst when we come back from any journey we have to stand and ponder as to the exact position of our home. It is misery to find our way up to work again for we stumble into one another, over rope rollers and against tram sides. That journey makes us feel that we hate the colliery, almost hate one another. This winter is going to be different in some ways from the last however for as promptly as night comes so also does the grr-r-ring drone of the enemy planes rise and fall along the valley. Night after night they come almost to the same time. We can hear them above whilst we are having tea or supper, sounding more plain than the buses that pass outside. Often we feel they must be touching the treetops and we wonder is a man right above us preparing to drop a bomb that will mean the end of our home and our lives.

There are preparations now, however, because the night sky is stabbed by fingers of light pointing out into the clouds. They swing and meet over the valley – a wonderful sight. We can see the searchlights from Cardiff, and from Barry over the one mountain, and from Swansea and Port Talbot over another and the lights from our own valley-end mingle with them to make a pattern of lights slicing the moving darkness of the clouds.

That is the atmosphere in which we stumble to work, with the sky lit up and the ground darkened. With our hearts weary with the dread that our homes may not be there when morning comes and we return. With the knowledge that we who have lived all our working days in danger must now feel that it is safer to be in the mine than the home and that the only place where we can walk with a light is into the bowels of the earth. The most dangerous place has become the safest – the worst lighted place is now the brightest. Thus has civilisation advanced into October 1940.

~

I noticed a fresh and very powerful searchlight last night – Tuesday night – a strange one. It seems to be coming from lower down the valley and it outlines the sycamores just above this house. Before the war the car lights used to light these trees up from the road and it was hardly necessary to carry a lamp. I was outside Tuesday night and an owl must have studied my movement, because it got high in the sycamore and started to mock at the feebleness of humanity. It was enjoying things nicely, so I believe, but I was not. Suddenly a brilliant streak of light flashed through the night and outlined the bird on a branch that was nearly bare. I was astonished for I had not seen that searchlight before; but my surprise was mild to that of the owl which found itself suddenly in the full glare. It checked itself halfway through a hoot and made a scrambling flutter through the tree branches into obscurity. Later I heard it renewing its complaints – but in a more subdued tone.

~

There is gloomy talk in this area. Miners are having notice and it is said that some collieries are closing down – and a month ago they were bombarding us for more coal and not the least lost time. I heard the miners' agent speaking and he was gloomy. We have better prospects at this colliery, so we are told, because there are sufficient inland orders to keep us going for twelve months so it is possible that we will work, although we may have some slack time. Had been asked to hand out leaflets advocating the election of our local secretary for a vacant position on the Miners' Executive.[35] Last Thursday at midday went to watch the day and afternoon shift at a Resolven colliery and hand the manifesto around. Hundreds of men were going to work, usually they came in crowds, making it difficult to detach leaflets fast enough for each one. One man who recognised me called across. 'Say Bert, why

[35] The Executive Council of the South Wales Miners' Federation.

don't you use an aeroplane.' That seemed a topical remark in view of our past actions in Germany.[36]

I was excused duty last night (Saturday) so stayed at home from the ambulance hall. About ten o'clock the guns began to rock the night and the sky seemed moving with raiders. Wife was paralysed with fright and Peter and I were pretty windy. The planes seemed circling continually above our house. I think they come back up here to gain height when the guns and searchlights drive them away. We thought there must be a half-a-dozen above us at the same time and as soon as one wave passed another zoomed over the mountains. We had the shutters tight closed but at last Peter and I went outside – a bad habit – so that we could see what was on and possibly have a chance to sidestep any bombs that might drop. We saw no bombs dropped but the night was moving with the drone of planes and the thud of guns. About two in the morning we were sleeping on our feet and both decided that they could bomb our house if they wished, we were going in to bed and we did. My last memories were of the roar of planes just above – then I woke to broad daylight – and still the planes were overhead. I looked out this time and discovered that these were friendly planes not the hawks of the night.

~

November, grey and dreary, with the trees all bare and the ferns brown on the mountains. Our thoughts are grey too for several collieries are closed and lines of loaded trucks stand in the siding, never moving. We are told that we will work as our inland orders are permanent – they go somewhere in the Lea Valley. Some men who have not long started are terribly anxious that they shall work another couple of weeks to get their twenty-six stamps on the card and so escape the means test if they are stopped. One of them has a family of evacuees with him, making thirteen in a small house. He says the woman and kids came to him after having a bad time but that she's clean and she slams in to help with the work so there'll be something for them as long as he's got a bite -- but he hopes to God he'll work another three weeks to get them twenty-six stamps.

[36] This is a reference to the fact that initial British bombing raids over Germany dropped propaganda leaflets rather than bombs.

~

Our little world has crashed, for a thousand and more men. We went to work as usual last Thursday night and were told – after our arrival – that there would be no more work until further notice.[37] We committee-men made inquiries, were assured again that orders were waiting in-plenty, but that the railway were 'acting the goat' and there was no prospect of work for a while. Just like that, no notice, no warning. It means the dole again and nothing for the first three days. Half the men will have to seek parish relief in a fortnight's time – they keep one week in hand at the office so we shall have money to draw next week. What would have happened had the men decided not to work? They would have been called lazy, and unpatriotic; it would have been counted an attempt to hinder the war effort. The company can stop you bang, just like that and we have no redress. Friday they gave every man a fortnight's notice but it is probable that not one day in that term will be worked. It's going to be awkward for the partially disabled men and I suppose that most of us who have worked long have some slight disability and very surely our chests are weakened by coal dust. Many of the men have made their homes lately and have bought furniture on easy payments – it's worrying them. Some few very thrifty ones are trying to pay for their houses – under our present system it would have been better for them to drink the money. The men lounge about the street corners, not knowing what to say or do. Claims for unemployment insurance have to be drawn up and the labour exchange seems quite unable to deal with the extra work. The clerks appear slow and new to their job. To improve it all the rain has not ceased for days. I tramped over two miles through the rain, waited for nearly three hours, then was told to come back next day. Raining next day and after a long wait was given a form which was to be returned next day. What utter stupidity, and how unsympathetic these officials are. Is it absolutely necessary for men to have a secondary education to become so stupid as some of these are? I guarantee that I will pick a like number of miners who will do this exchange job quicker, more efficiently, and more kindly, than the ones who

---

[37] There were widespread closures of anthracite-producing collieries in November and December 1940.

cause us to waste our days now. This walking wears out boots; bus fare is too expensive. Men are grumbling and I feel trouble is brewing. When we complained we were told curtly 'Why don't you write to your Minister of Labour about it?' Obviously a sneer at the appointment over them of a man whom they count of inferior class. Little hope of building a better Britain if men of that type are to be left in office – put them on a shovel, that would learn them manners.

~

I made six journeys before my claim to unemployment pay was put right and mine was an average case. So I walked more than twenty-four miles and got five soakings so that I should have fifteen shillings. I am positive that two journeys would have been ample. It is the slowest, crudest, method of handling men I have ever seen. Insulted and bullied by labour exchange clerks in this war for democracy and bombarded by enemy planes by night – we are having a good time. All men who were partially disabled because of accident at the colliery are now on the same basis as the other unemployed and must compete in the effort to obtain work with fit men. What chance have they? But to reclaim their partial allowance for the injuries they must prove that a prospective employer refused them work because of their injury. Employers are scarce and those who would admit that are scarcer still. It is a damnable position for the injured men and even when they were working every increase we had owing to the cost of living lessened the amount that they were paid because of their partial disability. Their earning capacity was counted on the wage-rate before war came and their disability assessed at that period. So each war increase would lessen the gap between their earnings before the accident and after it. Poor devils, some of them are very bitter. Their only shield is the trade union and the officials are fighting for them without cease. In one morning seventeen cases of serious disability were dealt with at our colliery.

~

We see men fetching their tools home from work every day now. These tools cost a lot to buy and may get buried if left inside long.

Also I see men, women and children scratching for coal in the tips whilst the rain is freezing on them. Facing me, as I write, is a mountain so full of coal that it crops out to the surface. Yet the people have empty grates – the ones whose fathers and grandfathers slaved and died to produce coal – and great profits, in the past. Yet we know that there are people who need this coal that is never taken away. In fact in this area where the coal dust kills men every day we are ourselves short of coal. Each miner who is a householder is entitled to a ton of coal a month at a reduced rate as part of his working privileges. The price for us is six shillings and eightpence a ton; with haulage it brings my load up to about thirteen shillings. This is what the price list says – one load a month – but getting it is another matter. In practice we are not allowed to order a free load until a month has passed since the last was delivered. Then they take very good care that a fortnight or three weeks pass before the coal is delivered so it hardly ever runs into more than two loads every three months. They delay sending the trucks down so that the hauliers can get at them or do other little tricks of a like sort because every load delayed is a saving for the company. Now, at our colliery we have a list of one hundred and nine men who have ordered coal and are properly entitled to it but cannot get it. We appealed to the company and asked them to let us have a few of the trucks that held about twelve hundred tons waiting on the sidings. Their reply was that those trucks had been weighed, labelled, and paid for, yet they were not moved for weeks – but we should not touch one. We asked to be allowed to work one day to get coal ready again for the houses, that was refused also. That is what is called co-operation. There could be no danger of loss to the company because each man had his holiday pay bonus in the company's books. I was so blazingly bitter about the whole muddle and the meanness that I sat down and wrote a letter to a great national weekly – with over a million circulation – to explain the whole situation as I saw it.[38] I had no fire in the house at the time. That afternoon I had heard Horner say they had tried every way of moving the owners' and the public's thoughts, but seemed to be up against a blank wall. I posted the letter, then

---

[38] Coombes wrote to *Picture Post*, and although this letter was not published, it led to his being invited to contribute to the special 'Plan for Britain' issue of 4 January 1941.

sat back and wondered was it any use? That day I had seen the terrible figures for silicosis in this area. We are in the Anthracite area, which is only a small section of the total mining area, but we have much more than half the silicosis and anthracosis victims here. This industrial disease is spreading so rapidly that it is getting to cost more to insure the miners against the disease than it costs to cut the coal – and unless they insure against it the law won't allow them to work a colliery – a wise precaution when one remembers that it used to be possible to wind up a colliery company and leave the injured workmen destitute.

Collieries idle all around, men standing about the corners or searching for coal in the tips and avoiding the police whilst we are continually exhorted to 'Go to it' – WHAT? Wireless still out of order so miss the news. Cannot get a paper without a regular order which is out of the question with us unless we want to walk two miles there and the same back to fetch it. When I have a chance I walk to the welfare library and have a real read – all the papers, then *John O'London, New Statesman, Tribune, Colliery Fireman,* and end up with the *Smallholder* as a sort of opening to another world.

~

Some news this weekend. Apparently they are going to move some of our coal and a part of our colliery may start tomorrow.[39] Only four hundred men will work instead of the thousand-odd. The big seams are to remain idle and the yard seams are to work. The awkward part is that the oldest hands nearly all work in the big seams and the yard is worked chiefly by men who have not worked for this company many years. The management seem indifferent, probably they would prefer, in some cases, that the newer hands were kept on but the workmen have their custom, which must be observed, in cases like this. Seniority must count; the oldest hands must have preference. Some men have worked here for fifteen and more years but the difficulty is that men have come and gone, and sometimes come back again and the management do not give the men's committee much help in the matter. It is sometimes the case

[39] From Christmas 1940 onwards the crisis in the anthracite industry eased and collieries reopened.

that a man is not working here for awhile and then starts back. Our rule is that length of service must count and after that the grade a man works in. Say that twenty repairers are needed, then they will be the men graded as repairers at the time of the stoppage who have been longest on the wage books. Had any one changed his job we would not be allowed to return to it and so displace another man, even if that man was a more recent worker. But remember that about seven hundred men must be idle and nearly everyone of those will feel that he has a grievance – and the only place where it can be redressed is by his committee. He feels there is no cause to be gentle in his language when explaining that grievance. In any case the present workers must be allowed to continue until the list is drawn up properly. 'Why is that?' some old hand will ask; 'it ought to be ready so that he shall not lose one day.' Useless to tell him that although the company can make the colliery idle when it likes the men's representatives have to be careful that proper notice is given to any man who must stop work because of seniority. Then the ones who are drawn out feel they have a grudge against the committee because they are compelled to stop. If they ask any questions of the management he tells them: 'It's not my doing – your Federation has drawn you out.' So after three days we got the exchange going and the old hands replacing the new. Then came the problem of men having to work in a strange seam and not being able to earn their money – and on top of it all, the management cut away all extra payments for work done. It was a horrible week and I can see our secretary ageing. He well earns that extra pound a week for looking after the affairs of a thousand men. The bitter part is that the men who are servile to the manager or official usually are the most blasphemous when dealing with their own secretary. Then the tricks they try on us, counting themselves clever if they succeed. No man must be penalised on his seniority because of illness and some try to claim that illness has caused their absence, until investigation proves they are lying. It often means a deal of work to prove the case – and one mistake is broadcast and the poor secretary is bombarded by the victims, his family, and all friendly relatives. We held our committee meetings with an impatient crowd outside the door. Two and three hours of argument inside and the same happening outside.

~

Another week of sifting and arguing over cases. One man proved that an eight years' absence was due to illness. One favourite with the management was idle for eight months. Management supports his claim that he was idle because there was no work for him in his grade. We cannot disprove that although we suspect an evasion. Another claimed that he knew one man – his mate – had been sacked and so should not have been given seniority over the accuser. Investigated, and found that the sacking meant sending home for one day because of an argument. Thus can a grievance be magnified and our time wasted.

It will soon be my time to restart. I have worked here fourteen years and I shall be the next repairer to start. Many labourers and other grades are working who have not worked here anything like so long but we cannot shuffle men about from one job to another in a crisis like this. It would be unfair for a labourer to have to give up his job to a higher paid man just for the period of depression. One thing shows clearly – that men are prepared to go to almost any length to keep such a poorly paid and risky job as mining because it gives them a few shillings a week more spending money than the dole.

Heard from *Picture Post*. Great surprise, apparently they want to use my letter and I shall hear more from them. They want to know about my family. We are buying a poor sort of house coal at the door – when we can get it – for two and sevenpence per hundredweight. Opposite me is a mountain so full of coal that it crops out to daylight and when we were allowed to work there the cutting price was two shillings a ton – all but a ha'penny. A man from Aberdare, a coal salesman, told me he can't get coal for his customers although he lives in an area where six collieries are idle. He told me the price was two pounds eight a ton – and we cut it for one and eleven pence ha'penny.

~

Started to work in the middle of this week. Because there was no place for me until Wednesday they will crop the bonus turn for the week. I have protested, forcibly, but there it is. The committee cannot prevent it and under the least excuse the company will deduct the bonus turn which is given because of the awkwardness of the shift. If a man's wife or child is dying and he stays with them for one night, or if his bus breaks down or arrives too late the company grabs the chance gladly and takes the bonus shift off him in addition to the one he has lost – this shift is only given to the night and afternoon men and as some consideration for the inconvenience to their family and themselves for the awkward hours.

I am now in a small seam, after twelve years in a big one. In the nine feet the roof was sometimes twenty feet above our head and the coal seam was scarcely ever less than nine feet in thickness. The 'squeeze' there was tremendous because such a thickness of coal was extracted and there was no way of packing the space tightly. The whole mountain always seemed to be moving around us and timber was snapping, steel arches bending, or great lumps of coal pouncing out all through each shift. We never went on our knees, which was consoling to Crush and Wattie, neither of whom are religious, but there were many times when we had to travel under great heights with loose stones above because there was no way of securing the place. A little stone falling from that height would break a bone in a man's body.

Here, as I am now, in the yard seam everything seems on a small scale. We have to keep our heads down and our backs arched. When off the main roadways we have to crawl on our knees and that bony structure does not believe in such a method of progress. Mine are swollen up and tender to each touch, even the trousers seem to hit them hard. Can hardly walk along the road, my legs are so stiff and I ache all over my body. Crush's wife has been rubbing olive oil in his legs – his opinion of the yard seam is profane. Coal-cutters and conveyors are working here and every breath is thickly laden with coal dust. There is not so much pressure in these seams, which is a good job because there is no way of hearing what the roof is doing. One thing that has affected me is the way that old mates greet one another. There are men working in this seam that knew me years ago and we have not seen much of one another lately. They recall old escapes from falls and the tricks played on officials with as much enjoyment as would schoolboys retell their school escapades. As one or two old hands start back each night there is a grand re-union, with inquiries about home conditions, absent mates, and quite an animated procession to take him to his new working place and offer the lend of any tools he may lack.

~

Last night, Saturday, was in the house by myself when I heard the squeal of a small car stopping outside the gate. Presently two large men emerged in like manner to sardines escaping from a tin. They came to our door – apparently wanted to see me privately. Were inspector and sergeant of police – in mufti – and wanted my outline of the *Picture Post* letter as the paper was going to send staff photographers in this area. That was a surprise. Quite friendly and courteous. Lumbered off after depressing the springs of our best chairs for over an hour. Have heard there is no work again next week in our colliery – so that four days will be my Christmas pay.

~

Went off early to the Labour Exchange last Monday, wife going to square up whilst I was absent. Waited the usual two hours, then returned to find wife flustered and two friendly photographers waiting my coming. *Picture Post* had arrived – just like that. They claimed a telegram had been sent to tell of their coming but I fancy that was a fairy tale. Anyway, we soon got pally. Peter arrived with the dog, Sam, and away we went to snap the sights of the area with Peter and myself included. Frost was white on the ground, and we snapped men and women and children scraping for bits of coal on the tips, whilst thousands of tons were standing in the sidings.

Took several pictures in Resolven and caused great alarm amongst the special police. Asked an old ash collector to stand with me for a picture. He was alarmed and I could see his brain quivering as he tried to think of an excuse, which was not needed for he was snapped before the first word was uttered. Returned to find that wife had done a deal of polishing but had only been able to find bread and cheese for dinner. Anyway it was a gay meal, after which more journeys for snaps. Wife begged a little butter for tea and things went well after which they took some interior snaps. They are staying overnight at an hotel in Neath as they want more pictures up at the other end of the vale. They arrived again next morning before we were ready and we started off for more pictures.

~

Christmas has gone again and for a wonder we have been almost a week without an enemy plane passing. Why this lull? We are almost as nervous when no raids come as when they are overhead because we fear some new form of attack. A pretty dreary Christmas for all in this area although the weather is mild and chrysanthemums are still blooming in a corner of the garden. We put up some holly and cut a log. Turkeys were three shillings a pound and we have never eaten turkey anyway. We had a small piece of beef and a pudding that tasted something like Christmas pudding. One carol singer came to our door – he got twopence. Had one visitor – a woman whose total conversation consisted of abuse for our next-door neighbour – some hundreds of yards away – because she would not spare her one onion and thus made it impossible for her to stuff the fowl. One of my mates brought me, very proudly, three tiny onions; half share of six which had been given him by another mate in return for the writing of a letter.

~

So here is civilisation in the year of 1941. Poor little forty-one, they haven't given much encouragement to you. Last Sunday night I re-started to work, don't expect we'll work many turns though. Monday afternoon I went down to the Exchange to sign for days lost last week. Altogether was away three hours and went nowhere else. My sleep lost and feeling stiff all over – if I doze off in work as a result will get fined and dubbed as lazy. Colliers from Resolven pits were there with their shirts soaking with sweat and their feet wet – they had to wait for nearly two hours in the cold before signing and went home with their teeth chattering – nearly six o'clock for some. Exactly the same happened on Wednesday, New Year's Day. After a long wait and many complaints one of the clerks repeated the taunt 'Why don't you write to your man – Bevin?' There'll be a real row there one day and somebody will get his dole stopped for insolence. I had one pound two and eightpence for self, wife and Peter to live on. They did not pay anything for two days during Christmas holidays. About time the dole was brought up to war time needs or the dole people realised that a war was on.

Our pictures in the *Post* yesterday. Locality apparently seething and piles of complaints that I was not talking to this one or that one or in this street or that street when I was snapped, paper shop had an extra hundred odd and they have gone whilst regular customers abuse the vendor for not keeping theirs. Promised to mind the house yesterday but went down to get the paper and was so long delayed by people who insisted on talking about the pictures and the letter that I was away four hours – and the fire was out when I got home. The feelings of wife and Peter coming home on a night of bitter frost to find me making desperate efforts to start a fire could not have been very pleasant. This Sunday morning the frost is severe and the leaves rustle when the birds move on them. The robin has been tapping at the window which is thick with frost. The paper boy has brought the Sunday papers: dear old *Reynolds* for our education and the *News of the World* in case we feel an interest in murder and seduction, and he says they have seen our picture and his father is going to get a frame to keep it in memory.[40]

~

1941 is now more than a week old. Monday night it was freezing severely. As we walked inside there was a frosty haze around the compressed air pipes even when they were a mile underground; funny thing they never get ice in the engines during the winter but they do during the summer – must be something to do with air condensation, I suppose. Icicles were hanging far inside the drift mouth. They looked like silver needles, giant white spikes, and were dangerous to anyone who did not bend low enough as they would spike their head or face. Not many years ago a journey rider was killed at his work by hitting his head against an icicle that was hanging down outside the drift arching. It is densely dark when we come home in the morning and we stumble along over slippery roads. I have to feel my way along the garden and around the back of the house. Enemy planes are over when we go in to work all this week and almost every morning they are around when we come out. I go into bed at eight in the morning whilst it is still dark and sleep until dinner time.

Many of the men who have been sent away to work have returned home and several are ill – one has died. I expected it

[40] *Reynolds* refers to *Reynolds News*, a left-wing Sunday paper.

because the weather has been severe and the men were used to working inside in a warm seam; besides nearly all of them have chests that are weakened by dust inhalation. Their wives were uneasy too, as they were left, often with several children to guard during the raids. Many of the men helped in the home and were useful, for when there are three or four toddlers the wife is not able to run messages or do much work and how she would handle them if a bomb fell near takes some imagining. Many of the men complain that they were only working part time and that whenever a dispute threatened the military were called out to them with fixed bayonets. Talking to two mates who were away in the RAMC they have mixed with Canadians and their views have altered.[41] They are intensely democratic now – no more upper class for them. They avow it will all have to be altered after this war – I hope they're right. They seem insistent enough and claim that their mates feel the same.

We are elated by the great victory at Bardia and it seems we and Greece have altered the swing of events.[42] Good work. The wireless doctor has just been here. He has informed me gravely that although there seemed plenty of life in our set he couldn't get a sound out. I would rather plenty of sound and no life. Apparently the set has been 'struck dumb'. He has not yet suggested we buy a new set – that is reserved for a later visit – I suppose.

[41] Royal Army Medical Corps.
[42] Bardia, in Italian-held Libya, was captured by the British Western Desert Force on 5 January 1941, with the surrender of forty-five thousand Italian troops. Greece had been successful in repulsing the Italian invasion which had begun on 28 October 1940.

FURTHER READING

Works by B. L. Coombes

B. L. Coombes, *These Poor Hands: The Autobiography of a Miner Working in South Wales* (Cardiff: University of Wales Press, 2002 edn, eds Bill Jones and Chris Williams).
Those Clouded Hills (London: Cobbett Publishing Company, 1944).
Miners Day (London: Penguin, 1945).

Studies of Coombes

Christopher M. Baggs, 'A "war-time mirror to Welsh life"? B. L. Coombes and the *Neath Guardian*', *Morgannwg* 34 (1990).
'Coombes, Bert Lewis', entry in *Dictionary of Labour Biography Vol.IV*, ed. Joyce M. Bellamy and John Saville (London and Basingstoke: Macmillan, 1977).
Bill Jones and Chris Williams, *B. L. Coombes* (Cardiff: University of Wales Press, 1999).
Bill Jones and Chris Williams, 'The B. L. Coombes Archive', *Welsh Writing in English* 5 (1999).
Paul Lester, 'By these poor hands: the writings of B. L. Coombes', *London Magazine* 33, Nos.9–10 (1993–4).
David Smith, 'Underground man: the work of B. L. Coombes, "miner writer" ', *The Anglo-Welsh Review* 24, No.53 (1974).
Keith Gildart, 'Mining memories: reading coalfield autobiographies', *Labour History*, 50 (2009), 139–61.
Barbara Prys-Williams, *Twentieth-Century Autobiography* (Cardiff: University of Wales Press, 2004).

Studies of the South Wales Coalfield

Hywel Francis and David Smith, *The Fed: A History of the South Wales Miners in the Twentieth Century* (2nd edn, Cardiff: University of Wales Press, 1998).

Bill Jones and Beth Thomas, *Coal's Domain / Teyrnas y Glo* (Cardiff: National Museum of Wales, 1993).

Ioan Matthews, 'The world of the anthracite miner', *Llafur: Journal of Welsh Labour History / Cylchgrawn Hanes Llafur Cymru* 6, No.1 (1992).

Chris Williams, 'The South Wales Miners' Federation', *Llafur: Journal of Welsh Labour History / Cylchgrawn Hanes Llafur Cymru* 5, No.3 (1990).

Chris Williams, *Capitalism, Community and Conflict: The South Wales Coalfield, 1898–1947* (Cardiff: University of Wales Press, 1998).

Sue Bruley, *The Women and Men of 1926: A Social and Gender History of the General Strike and Miners' Lockout in South Wales* (Cardiff: University of Wales Press, 2010).

Steven Thompson, *Unemployment, Poverty and Health in Interwar South Wales* (Cardiff: University of Wales Press, 2006).